Vehicle Body Engineering

Dr. A K BABU
Associate Professor
Department of Automobile Engineering
SRM Easwari Engineering College
Chennai-600089, Tamilnadu, INDIA

KHANNA PUBLISHING HOUSE
NEW DELHI (INDIA)

Dear Readers,

To prevent the piracy, this book is secured with HIGH SECURITY HOLOGRAM on the front title cover. In case you don't find the hologram on the front cover title, please write us to at contact@khannabooks.com or whatsapp us at +91-99109 09320 and avail special gift voucher for yourself.

Specimen of Hologram on front Cover title:

Enlargement Of Overlay

Moreover, there is a SPECIAL DISCOUNT COUPON for you with EVERY HOLOGRAM.

How to avail this SPECIAL DISCOUNT:

Step 1: Scratch the hologram
Step 2: Under the scratch area, your "coupon code" is available
Step 3: Logon to www.khannabooks.com
Step 4: Use your "coupon code" in the shopping cart and get your copy at a special discount
Step 5: Enjoy your reading!

ISBN: 978-93-90779-01-7

Vehicle Body Engineering
by Dr. A.K. Babu

First Edition: 2021
Reprint: 2026

Published by:
Khanna Book Publishing Co. (P) Ltd.
CIN: U22110DL1998PTC095547

Visit us at: **www.khannabooks.com**
Write us at: **contact@khannabooks.com**

To view complete list of books, Please scan the QR Code: KPH

Printed by Bharat.

Preface

This handy book has been designed for easy reading and to meet the vital requirements of students in the branches of Automobile Engineering. It is based on the latest syllabi prescribed by different technical colleges and Universities in India.

The approach of this informative book is completely different from other books of the same title available in the market. The contents are presented in six concise chapters. Each chapter describes important concepts in simple, easy to comprehend non-technical language, and shows with the aid of clear illustrations how vehicle body parts and systems are constructed, how the parts work, and what is required to maximize performance in terms of power, speed, economy and safety.

The illustrations are easy to follow and fully meet the requirements of our exam oriented education system. The important short and long review questions are included at the end of each chapter to enable self-testing. These questions are compiled from question papers of previous semesters, covering various technical colleges and Universities. This comprehensive question bank will greatly assist students in identifying the important topics they need to focus on to be able to do their best in examinations.

This course book is intended for use as a Textbook and as a primary Reference book by colleges and technical universities offering subjects like Vehicle Body Engineering and Auto Body & Repair.

I welcome comments or suggestions that will help me further improve the book in subsequent editions. Any feedback will be greatly appreciated.

Acknowledgements

Acknowledgements for this book are difficult to make because many books and manuals have influenced me directly or indirectly in its preparation. Therefore, I wish to express my grateful thanks to all the concerned authors, publishers and manufacturers.

The authors would also like to thank Khanna Book Publishing Pvt Ltd, New Delhi for their time and effort in ensuring the excellent appearance of the book with clear text, handy size, neat finish and reasonable price.

AUTHOR

Contents

1 Introduction

Vehicle body engineering provides knowledge about construction of car body, bus body, commercial vehicle details, ground vehicle aerodynamics, body materials, body trim, mechanisms and modern painting process.

VEHICLE WEIGHTS AND DIMENSIONS

Major weights and dimensions of a vehicle are explained below:

WEIGHTS

Payload

The total weight of passengers and cargo that a vehicle carries or can carry.

Gross Vehicle Weight (GVW)

GVW is the weight of the vehicle, plus the weight of all passengers the vehicle is designed to carry, plus the maximum allowable payload (passengers and cargo) or luggage load.

Curb Weight (CW) or Kerb Weight (KW)

CW is the weight of a vehicle wet, meaning with a full tank of fuel and all fluids filled, but without passengers or cargo (luggage).

Model Weight (MW)

MW is the weight of a vehicle wet and with passengers.

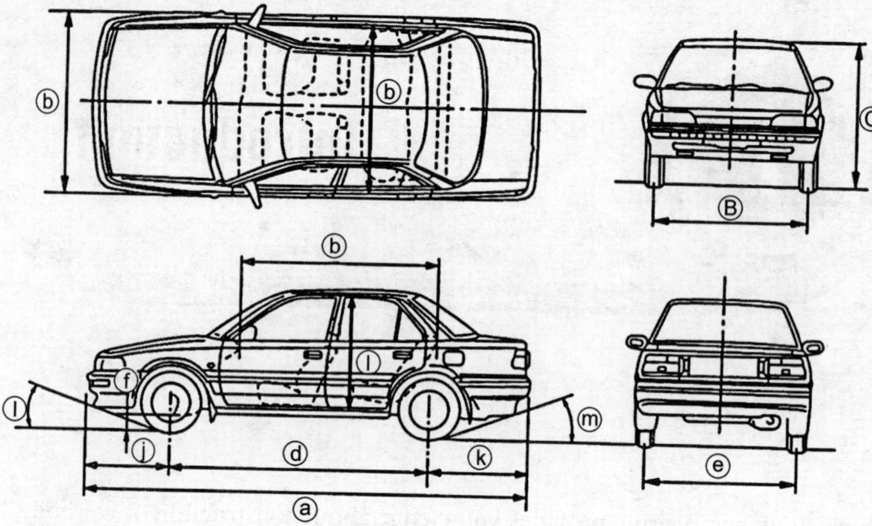

Fig.1.1: Vehicle weights and dimensions

DIMENSIONS

(a) Overall length

The distance between the front and rear of the vehicle measured along the longitudinal centre line, including bumper guards, if the vehicle has them.

(b) Overall width

The maximum lateral distance measured between the sides of the vehicle. It includes bumpers, moldings, sheet metal protrusions, etc., measured to the outside of the metal.

(c) Overall height

The maximum vertical distance from the top of the roof to the road surface, measured with the vehicle in a curb weight condition.

(d) Wheelbase

The distance between the center lines of the front and rear axles.

(e) Tread

The distance between the center lines of tyres.

(f) Minimum running ground clearance

The minimum clearance measured from ground with the vehicle in a gross vehicle weight condition.

(g) Room length

The horizontal distance along the vehicle's longitudinal (lengthwise) center line from the top of the instrument safety pad to the point directly above the top of the rear seatback.

(h) Room width

The maximum lateral distance between the trimmed interior body surfaces.

(i) Room height

The maximum vertical distance from the top of the floor covering to the headlining.

(j) Overhang-front

The distance from the center line of the front wheels to the front of the vehicle, including bumper guards if they are standard equipment.

(k) Overhang-rear

The distance from the center line of the rear wheels to the rear of the vehicle, including bumper guards if they are standard equipment.

(l) Angle of approach

The angle formed by the ground and the line tangent to the front tyre static loaded radius arc and the first point of interference (i.e. bumper, guard, gravel deflector, fender or other components excluding license plate).

(m) Angle of departure

The angle formed by the ground and the line tangent to the rear tyre static loaded radius arc and the first point of interference (i.e. bumper, guard, gravel deflector, tail pipe, fender or other components excluding license plate).

2 Car Body Details

The car body has four main functions:

1. Protect the occupants and cargo.
2. Provide attachment points for all other major components and manage the stress between them.
3. Provide an appealing appearance for the vehicle.
4. Provide an aerodynamic shape to improve performance and reduce noise.

CAR BODY ASSEMBLY

A car body can be divided into three main groups of assemblies: underbody, upperbody and closures.

Underbody

The underbody consists mainly of the floor panels and dash structure which are stiffened by a number of box sections to form a substructure. These box sections comprise the main longitudinal frame rails, the sills and the cross members. The chassis components are attached to this substructure which also serves as the primary crash structure, running out to the extremities of the body.

Upperbody

The upper body can be a framework surrounding a series of apertures and supporting the outer skin of the vehicle. Each aperture or opening is designed to provide access into the vehicle or visibility out of it.

Closures

The closures include the doors, hood and truck lid/tailgate. These represent a large portion of the exterior surface.

TYPES OF CAR BODY

Cars can be identified by their body styles and size. Body styling has to accommodate passengers and luggage space, power train, steering, suspension and wheels, etc. The following are some of the important body styles used for cars.

Saloon (or) Sedan

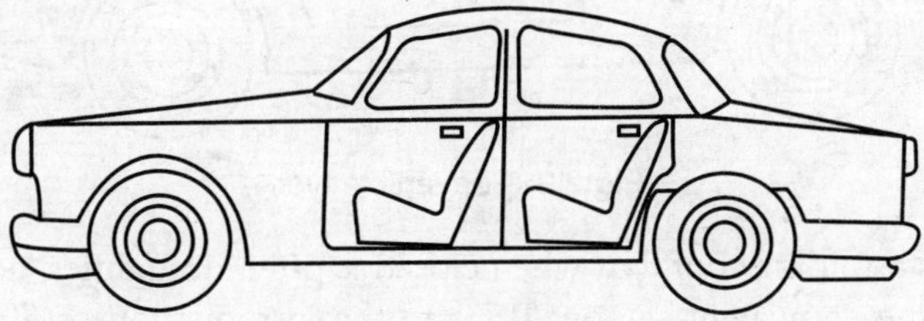

Fig.2.1: Saloon

The basic car body shape is the saloon, with two or four doors and a luggage compartment at the front or rear. The shape of body shell is based on three 'boxes'. The front box forms the engine compartment, the centre section the container for the occupants and the rear box a storage space, called a boot (trunk) for the luggage.

This type has the features such as well designed seats, ease of entry and exit, good air-conditioning system and better styling.

Examples

Honda City, Hyundai Verna, Tata Indigo, Volkswagon Vento etc.

Hatchback (or) Lift back

This type is half-way between a saloon and an estate car. The distinguishing feature of this type of vehicles is their rear luggage compartment, which is an extension of the passenger compartment. Access to the luggage compartment is gained through an upward opening hatch door from which this type of vehicle derives its name. This type of vehicles comes in 3 and 5-door versions.

Fig.2.2: Hatchback

Examples

Honda Brio, Maruti Alto, Hyundai Eon, etc.

Convertible (or) Drop-head coupe

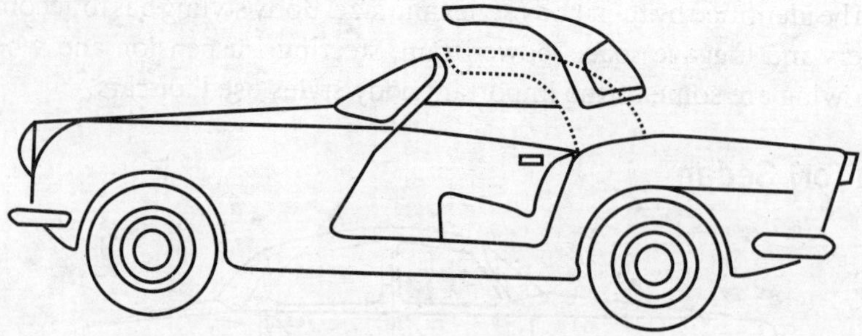

Fig.2.3: Convertible type

This type has a folding roof, but when closed is often draughtier, noisier and less roomy than the equivalent saloon. Prior to the introduction of air-conditioning this type was widely used in hot countries.

The roadster is a two-seat car with folding roof, the latest versions having a clip-on fibreglass roof. The convertible limousine has limousine size and finish with a fixed partition but a folding roof. Sliding roofs are now popular on standard saloon cars. Sports cars with fold-flat windscreens are called torpedoes or spyders.

Examples

Porche Boxster, Audi A3, BMW Z4, etc.

Coupe

It is a small car with two seats, for a driver and a passenger. It has better aerodynamic shape and better acceleration. Styling is not much important. Lightness combined with rigidity is the special feature.

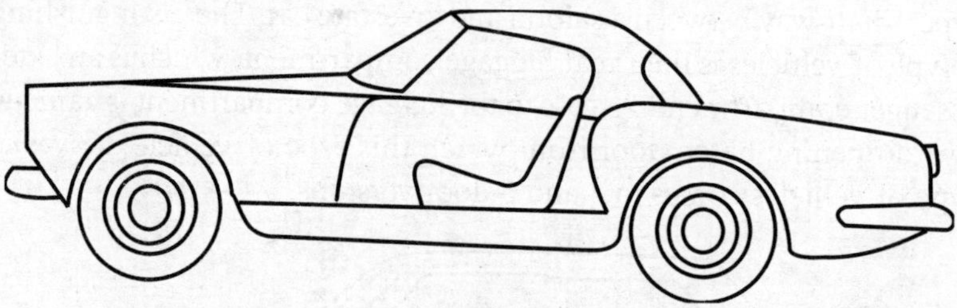

Fig.2.4: Coupe

Today some coupe models are called '2+2'. This generally suggests that the rear seat accommodation is rather cramped for adults but is suitable for children or for occasional adult use.

Examples

Audi TT, Porsche Cayman, BMW M4, etc.

Estate car

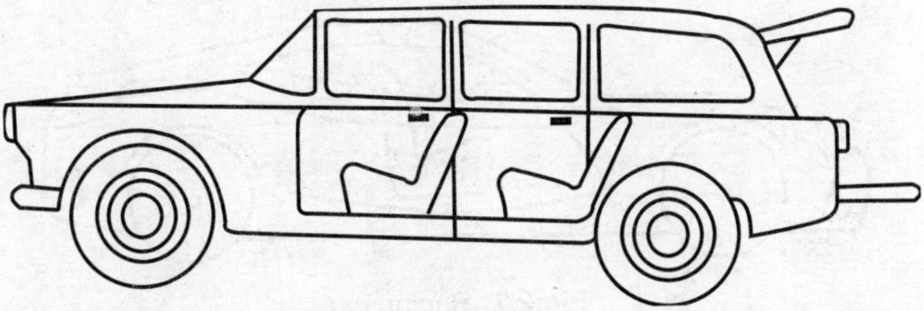

Fig.2.5: Estate car

The estate car is also known as universal, kombi, station wagon, camping, break, etc. It has the luggage space as a continuation of the passenger compartment. The rear door, which can be opened in various ways depending on the model, provides access to the luggage compartment. Folding the rear seats down gives a larger floor area for the carriage of luggage or goods. Stronger suspension springs are fitted at the rear to support the extra load. Station wagons come in 2 and 4-door versions. More luggage space and longer wheel base are specialty. Used for touring, picnics, etc.

Examples

Tata Estate, Tata Indigo Marino, Fiat Palio Adventure, Volkswagen Passat Wagon, etc.

Limousine

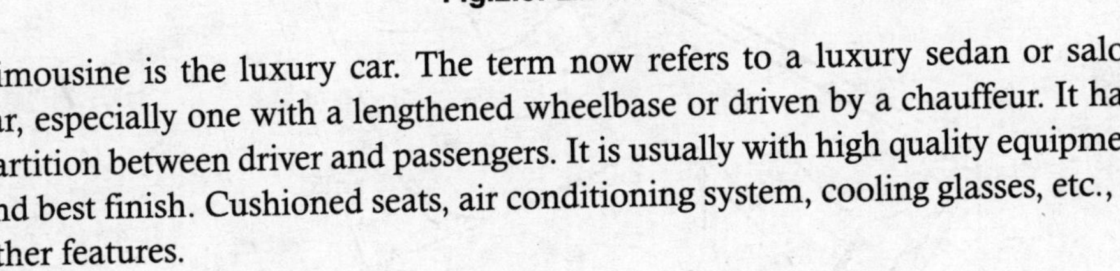

Fig.2.6: Limousine

Limousine is the luxury car. The term now refers to a luxury sedan or saloon car, especially one with a lengthened wheelbase or driven by a chauffeur. It has a partition between driver and passengers. It is usually with high quality equipments and best finish. Cushioned seats, air conditioning system, cooling glasses, etc., are other features.

Examples

The Beast, Rolls Royce Phantom Limo, The American Dream, Mercedes Benz S-600 Pullman, etc.

Racing and sports car

Fig.2.7: Racing car

Two prime criterias for racing cars are (1) lightness coupled with rigidity regardless of comfort and (2) body design must comply with the rules of the race or event such as length, width and height of car, engine capacity, fuel capacity, etc. Better aerodynamic shape is the unique feature of this design.

Examples

Lamborghini Huracan, Aston Martin Vantage, Porsche 911, etc.

VISIBILITY

Excellent visibility is one of the important requirements for vehicle safety. Driver visibility is the maximum distance at which the driver of a vehicle can see and identify prominent objects around the vehicle. Visibility is primarily determined by weather conditions and by a vehicle's design.

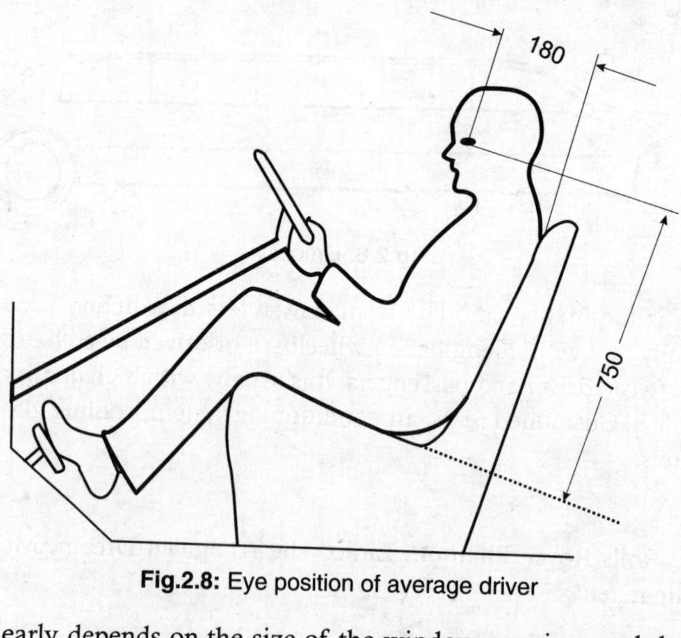

Fig.2.8: Eye position of average driver

This clearly depends on the size of the window openings and their position relative to the occupants.

Forward visibility

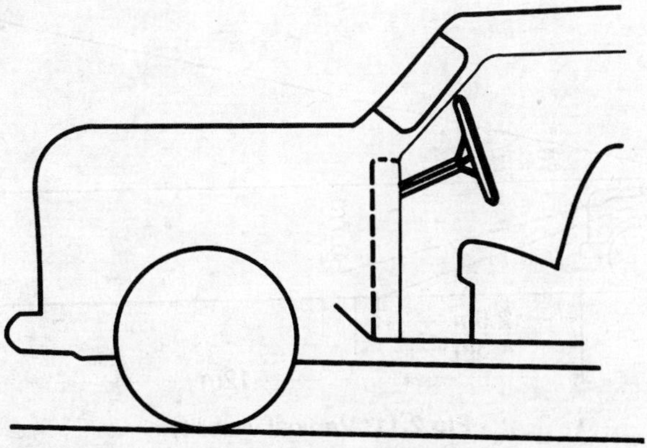

Fig.2.9: Forward visibility

If the occupant is placed close to the windscreen, the forward visibility is considerably improved. Ease of entry is possible by suitably shaping the door as shown by dotted line.

Downward visibility

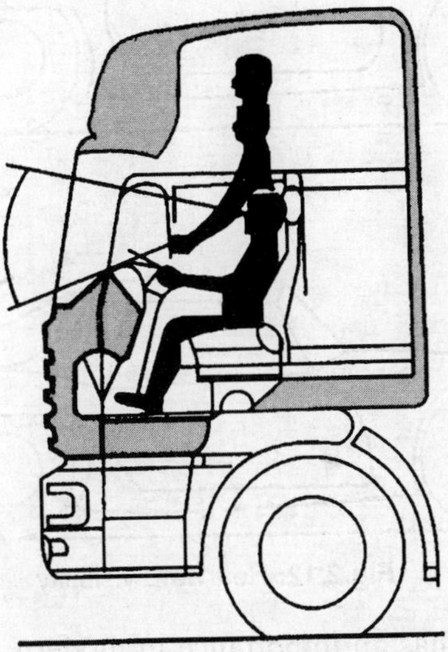

Fig.2.10: Visibility in military vehicles

In military vehicles the downward visibility is important and the driver must be positioned as high as possible in relation to the lower edge of the windscreen.

Vertical visibility

The upward angle of vertical visibility should enable the driver to see traffic lights, etc. and this must be taken into consideration at the design stage.

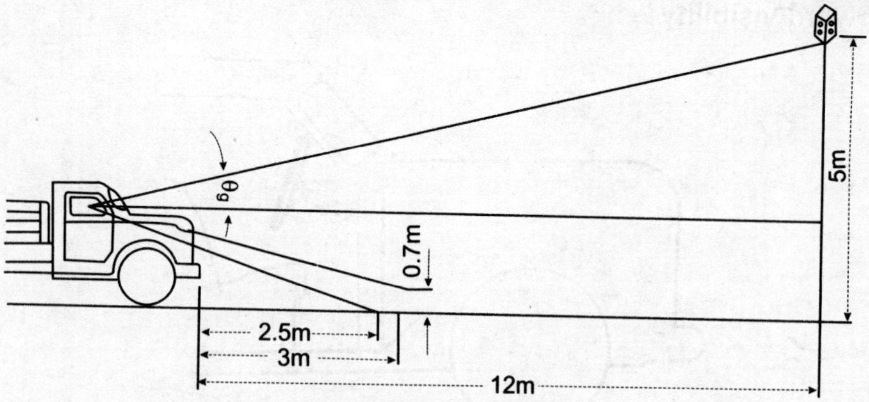

Fig.2.11: Vertical visibility

Rearward visibility

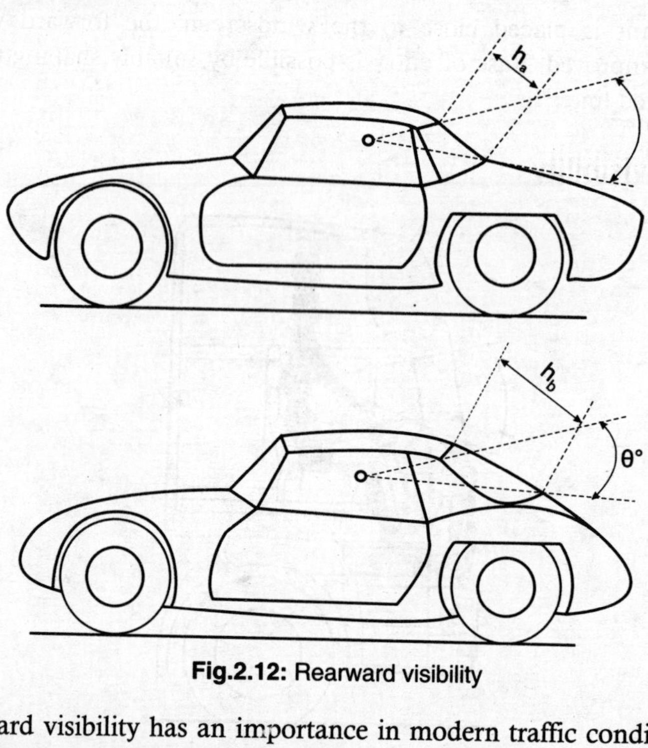

Fig.2.12: Rearward visibility

Rearward visibility has an importance in modern traffic conditions and the increase in glass area ($h_b > h_a$) required to maintain a given rear view vertical angle with a "fast-back" window as shown in Fig.2.12.

VISIBILITY REGULATIONS

Several international attempts have been made to prepare regulations for vehicle design which will be common to all countries. There are no strict regulations regarding visibility.

The essential requirements of visibility of a vehicle are given as below:

- The driver should be able to view out of the vehicle through a windscreen of adequate size.
- The obstruction of the non-transparent parts should not exceed given limits. No structural part should be present in front of the eyes of the driver, except the two A-pillars. Similarly, the hood, doors and the roof should not limit too much the possibility to view out of the vehicle.
- The number of pillars in front of the driver must not be larger than two, reducing the direct field of view by creating fields of obstruction.

IMPROVEMENTS IN VISIBILITY

Good driver visibility is essential to safe road traffic. A good view of everything around the vehicle is an integral aspect of the ergonomics of the driver's working area. Good visibility should be incorporated at the design stage (pillars, window frame members etc.) and maintained during driving by efficient ventilation and heating systems that keep the windows clear.

Visibility can be divided into two aspects: ability to see and to be seen.

Ability to see

1. By placing driver close to the windscreen, the forward visibility is considerably improved (Fig.2.9).
2. The downward visibility can be improved by positioning the driver as high as possible in relation to the lower edge of the windscreen (Fig.2.10).
3. To improve visibility, cabs should be designed to avoid 'blind spots' and to reduce headlight glare.
4. Visibility angles must be widened, in addition to front and rear visibility. Flashers on the side must considerably increase the chance of seeing a vehicle sideways on.
5. To help maintain good visibility through all of the windows by way of an appropriate rate of air throughput inside the vehicle. This prevents the build-up of damp, humid air which could cause condensation on the inner surface of the windows.
6. One of the major characteristics of automotive glazing is better visibility. But it must be remembered that an increase in glazed area results in reduced strength of the vehicle body structure.
7. The obstruction of the non-transparent parts should not exceed given limits. No structural part should be present in front of the eyes of the driver, except the two A-pillars. Similarly, the hood, doors and the roof should not limit too much the possibility to view out of the vehicle.
8. The number of pillars in front of the driver must not be larger than two, reducing the direct field of view by creating fields of obstruction.

Ability to be seen

1. In daylight colour is the most important characteristic in making cars more easily visible. Colours that are best from this point of view have to be recommended to the users.
2. Glitter also makes a car more visible as well as more attractive.

PARAMETERS INFLUENCING VISIBILITY

Parameters influencing the visibility characteristics of a particular vehicle include:

a. Location, size and shape of windows
b. Location, size, shape and attitude of mirrors and reflecting surfaces
c. Location of the point and eye range contour as determined by the vehicle seat position
d. Reflective coefficient of rear-vision mirrors, windows and windshields
e. Illumination intensity and pattern of vehicle headlights and back-up lights
f. Overall size and general geometry of vehicle, and
g. Modification of vehicle attitude due to loading

Measurements required to obtain sufficient data for determination of the above parameters include:

a. Physical location of the driver's viewpoint with regard to all windows, windshields and mirrors.
b. Solid angles of visibility as measured from driver's viewing point for all windows, mirrors, defogged areas, and wiped areas.
c. Geometric pattern and photometric intensity of headlight beams and back-up lights.
d. Photometric measurements of glare from driver's viewing point, and
e. Qualitative evaluation and specific location of glare sources as determined by driver's observations.

VISIBILITY TESTS

The primary objectives of vehicle visibility testing are:

a. Determination of forward and rear visibility angles and areas for a statistical distribution of normal driver eye-range contours.
b. Determination of factors which affect normal driving visibility and which might be modified so as to improve the vehicle's visibility characteristics.
c. Quantitative and qualitative measurement of glare as seen from the driver's viewing point
d. Determination of headlight illumination intensity and pattern, and

e. Interpretation of visibility data with regard to vehicle functional requirements, and the effect of visibility on the safety of the vehicle's operation in normal driving modes.

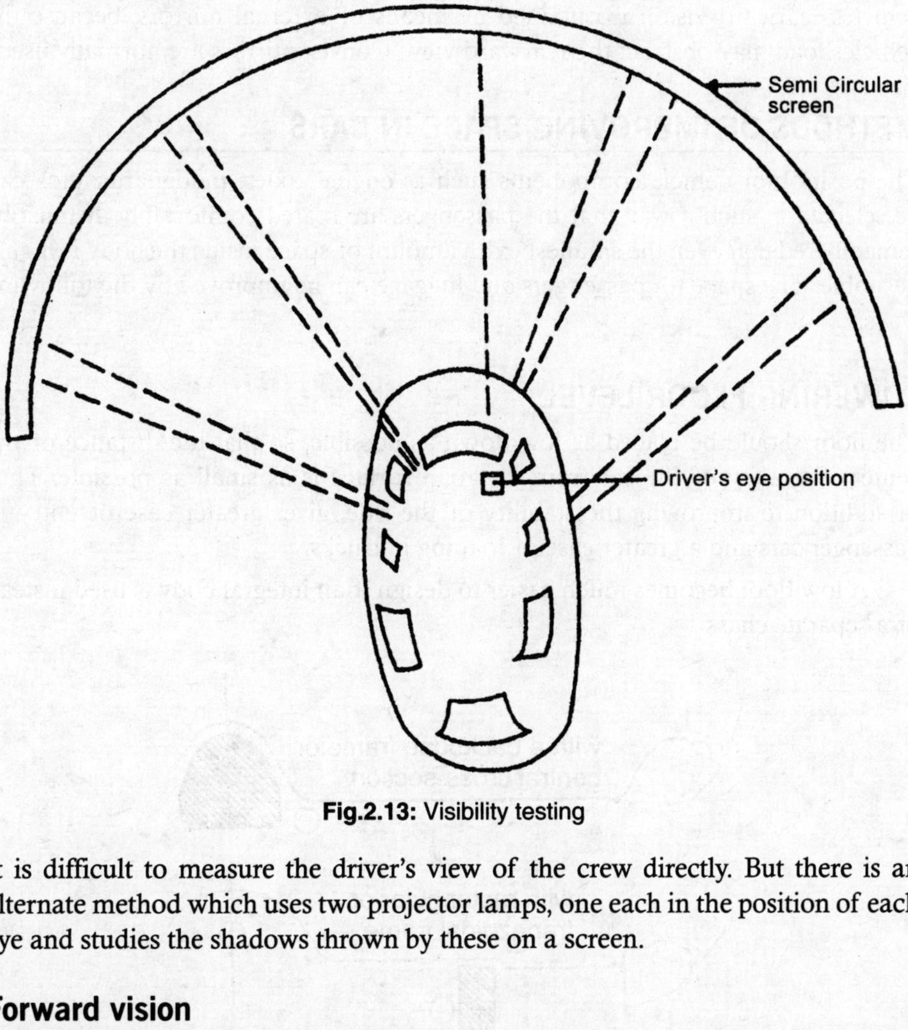

Fig.2.13: Visibility testing

It is difficult to measure the driver's view of the crew directly. But there is an alternate method which uses two projector lamps, one each in the position of each eye and studies the shadows thrown by these on a screen.

Forward vision

The vehicle is positioned facing a semi circular visibility screen, so that the midpoint of the driver's eyes lie on the cylindrical axis of the screen. The vehicles longitudinal axis is parallel to the horizontal bisection of the screen. The eyes are positioned on the base diameter of this screen. The areas visible to the driver are outlined by the shadows of the windscreen pillar and wiper sections etc. on the screen when the lamps are switched on.

Rearward visibility

Light from the lamps is reflected by the mirror and falls on two plane screens placed parallel to each other and perpendicular to vertical axis at a convenient distance behind the eyes. The area illuminated on each of these screen is a development of the shadow of the reflecting mirror or of the back light, so that it is useful to be able to identify the coordinates of the identifiable points are obtained separately from both screens and used to plot the ground plan of rearward vision. In commercial vehicles rearward vision is obtained by means of external mirrors, because the vehicles load may obstruct the rearward view. Convex mirrors are normally used.

METHODS OF IMPROVING SPACE IN CARS

The position of vehicle components such as engine, axles, mudguards, etc., can be selected in such a way that the passengers are seated comfortably. It must be remembered that even the smallest extra amount of space inside the body is highly desirable. The space for passengers and luggage can be improved by the following ways.

LOWERING FLOOR LEVEL

The floor should be placed as low down as possible, so that the distance of the center of gravity of the car from the road surface is as small as possible. This, in addition to improving the stability of the ride, gives greater ease of entry in passenger cars and a greater ease of loading in trucks.

A low floor becomes much easier to design if an integral body is used instead of a separate chassis.

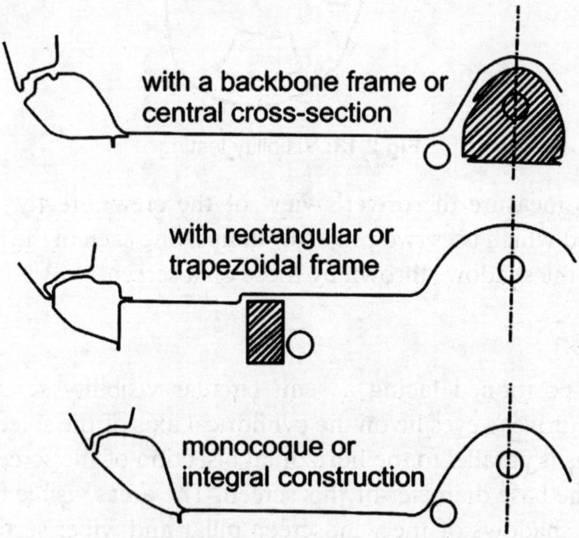

Fig.2.14: Floor level of a saloon car

POSITION OF SPARE WHEEL

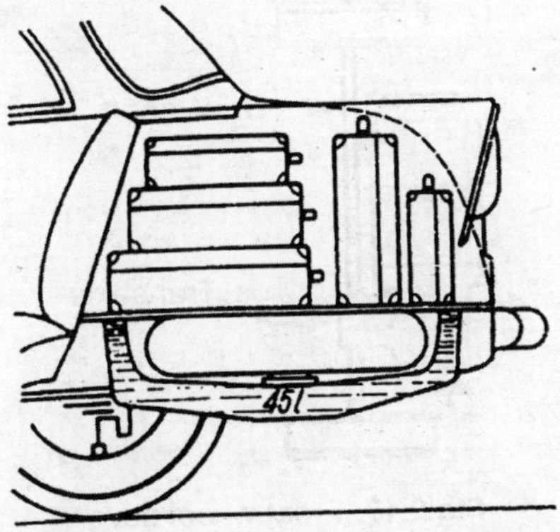

Fig.2.15: Spare wheel near fuel tank

As touring necessitates taking a large amount of luggage, the spare wheel is often placed near the fuel tank now-a-days as shown in Fig.2.15, thus obtaining an even greater boot capacity through increased width.

Transferring the spare wheel from the boot to the engine compartment (Fig.2.16) makes the available luggage capacity even greater. When trying to achieve a large boot, it is even possible to place the spare wheel outside the car, as in the Jeeps.

Fig.2.16: Spare wheel in bonnet

COMPACT DESIGN

Compactness of design is particularly important in small and medium sized passenger cars. This makes for good utilization of space and produces a smaller car which is also lighter, resulting in an improved power-to-weight ratio. Thus a less expensive car with better performance is obtained.

The space available in the passenger car depends on the position of the engine and transmission, and also on the overall height.

Front wheel drive

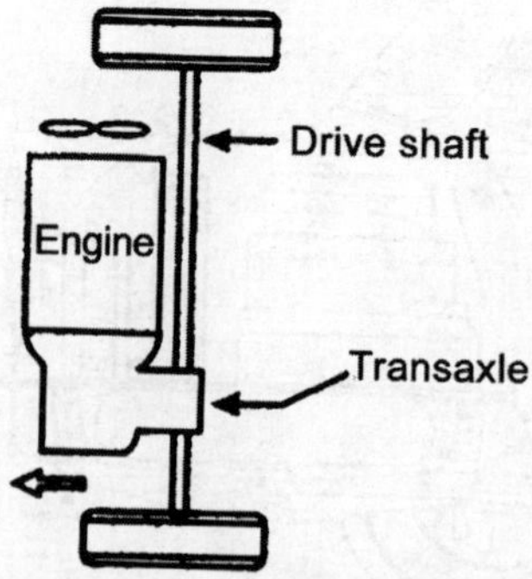

Fig.2.17: Front wheel drive

The compactness of this layout has made it very popular for use on passenger cars. The vehicle has both the engine and transaxle in the front. Accommodating all the main components under the bonnet (hood) in one compartment give maximum space within the car for the occupants, also the absence of floor bulges and tunnel provides more room for the rear passengers.

Rear engine

The space vacated by the engine at the front end can be used for passengers. This design also provides more space for the driver's leg.

Fig.2.18: Rear engine vehicle

DRIVER SEAT DESIGN

A correct driving position is important in the vehicle layout, and the seat position in relation to the steering wheel, foot controls and other secondary controls is of fundamental importance in body design. Seating position has an influence not only on the driver's comfort but also on road safety.

The following general points are to be considered in designing the driver's seat.

- Driver has to use his eyes to obtain at least 90% of the information he needs for driving safely. As regards the position of the seat itself, this must be such that his view of the scene outside the car is obstructed as little as possible by components such as rear view mirrors or windscreen pillars. Similarly his view of the instruments, switches and other controls must be clear.

- Driver must be able to reach all his controls easily, with a minimum of effort, and without being distracted from what is happening on the road ahead. Visibility of indicator and warning lamps under bright sunlight may cause the driver fail to notice. All controls should be easy to operate, and instrument and other indicators easy to read.
- The driver's seat should be adjustable 45 mm horizontally and 30 mm vertically.
- The most comfortable position of the body is achieved when the bulk of the weight of the seated person is taken by the ischial bones. A more slanted body position will cause abnormal tension in the pelvis muscles, leading to tiredness.
- The seat cushions should be fairly rigid and must have sufficient shock absorbing qualities to prevent resonance of any springs that may be incorporated.
- The back-rest supports the trunk in a vertical position and that the upper part of the back-rest support the upper portion of the spine and ensures the correct position of the trunk, with a pushed out and extended thorax and the shoulders slightly lowered. An uncomfortable back-rest results in compression of the thorax, which makes breathing difficult.
- A good back-rest relieves the neck and shoulder muscles and must depend on the size of the individual. Thus it is advisable to use an adjustable back-rest.
- The angle between the seat and back-rest must be obtuse. It is less for the driver than for the passenger seats.
- Armrests reduce tiredness if their position does not cause the trunk to bend or stretch.
- It is important to avoid acute angles between the trunk and pelvis, since the knees become raised and the thighs press on the stomach. This can be caused by any of the following:
    1. the seat being tilted too much
    2. insufficient room for the legs
    3. an unsuitable angle between the seat and back-rest.
- Numbness in the calves of the legs and in the feet is caused by the front edge of the seat exerting too great a pressure on the lower part of the thigh. This results from excessive height of the seat or a hollow seat. It can be avoided by introducing an adjustable front edge to the seat, that is, a front edge that can be rotated to bring the weight of the feet and calves on to the floor.
- It should be noted that the driver will need to shift his position slightly during a long journey. This indicates that sufficient width for this movement should be provided.

Passenger car seat design

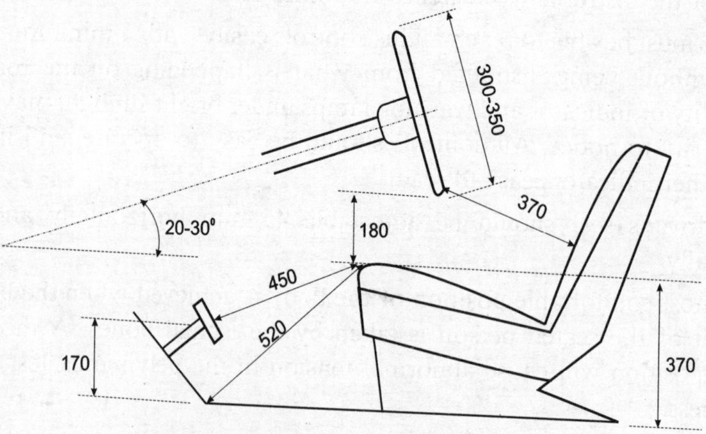

Fig.2.19: Dimensions of passenger car seat

Inclination of the steering column has a direct influence on the force which can be applied by the driver. A horizontal steering column used in car is designed for comfort. As it does not require the driver to use large forces, just the shoulders are involved in the work of turning the wheel.

Forces of varying magnitude can be exerted on the foot pedals, depending on the angles (α and β) of the inclination of the seat and back-rest. The distance between the floor and the seat also has some influence on these forces.

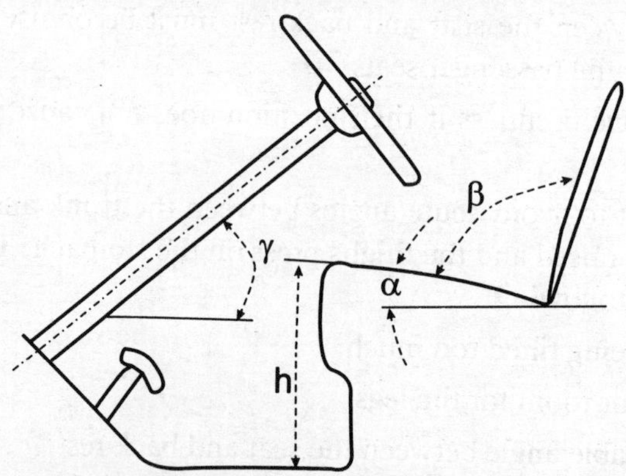

Fig.2.20: Seat and back-rest angles

Class of vehicle	Cushion height above floor, h mm	Angle of cushion inclination, °α	Angle of back-rest inclination, °β	Maximum force on pedal, P kg
Saloon	300-340	12	100	66

It should also be noted that harder seats allow the driver to use more force when controlling the vehicle.

CAR BODY CONSTRUCTION

REQUIREMENTS OF CAR BODY

A car body must satisfy requirements in terms of:

1. Strength
2. Stiffness
3. Space
4. Air drag
5. Protection against weather
6. Resistance to corrosion
7. Protection in accident

METHODS OF CONSTRUCTION

Basically there are three types of body structure: non-load carrying, semi-integral and integral.

Non-load carrying

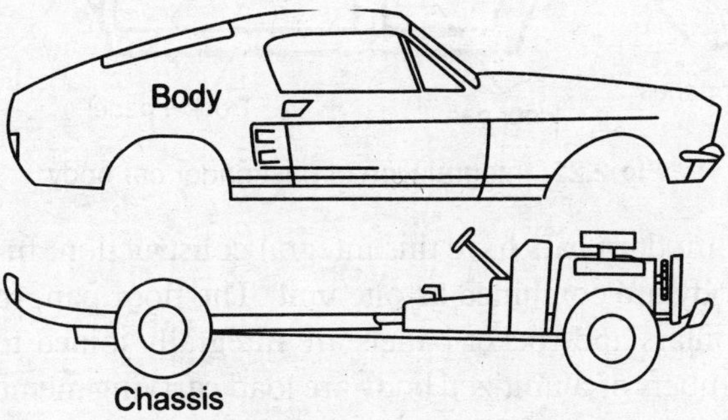

Fig.2.21: Non-load carrying

In this type, loads on the vehicle are transferred to the suspension entirely by a separate chassis. This type of construction was used in the early days of vehicle, the chassis frame carrying all loads and the bodywork either being made of very flexible material (wood) or being made stiff but isolated from the chassis deflection by body mountings, usually of rubber.

This type of construction is not used in passenger cars now-a-days because of the weight of the chassis frame and because of mounting problems where the loads in the bodywork were concentrated round the mountings, causing early failures.

Semi-integral type

When the body mounts are replaced by relatively stiff material that prevents squeaking due to the relative displacement between the body and the chassis, some of the load is transferred to the body structure and it becomes semi-integral. The amount of load carried by the body shell is clearly dependent on the number of attachments to the chassis and on the mount stiffness.

This type of construction is confined to small production cars. Such vehicles are heavy and assembly is difficult as small errors can introduce large forces into a body shell.

Integral type

Today, almost all passenger cars are of integral construction, also known as unitised body or frameless or monocoque construction.

In this type of construction heavy side members used in conventional construction are eliminated and the floor is strengthened by cross members and the body, all welded.

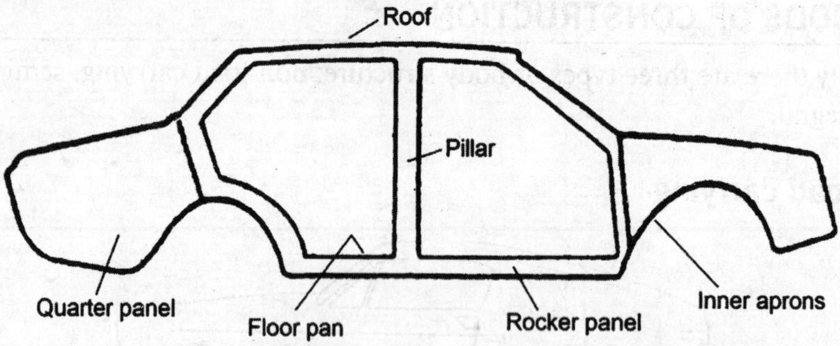

Fig.2.22: Integral type of passenger car body

Most of the modern cars have this integral construction. In this body design, the frame and body are combined as one unit. The floor pan, roof, inner aprons, quarter panels, pillars and rocker panels are integrally joined to form a unitized body. All the members of a unitized body are load carrying members. The unitized body spreads collision forces throughout the body to help protect the vehicle occupants.

Panels or members that share the load are called stressed panels. They have creases and bends to increase the strength. Unstressed panels are those that do not contribute significantly to the strength of the structure. Some of the components in a unitized body are made from high-strength steel (HSS) to provide additional protection in a collision.

The strength and rigidity of the unitized body is achieved by body design rather than by having a heavy steel frame to support the body. In this body design, body sheet metal is fabricated into a box design which provides good resistance to bending and torsion.

Advantages

1. Both lighter and stronger

2. Small number of components required
3. Ability to style the outer body panels as desired

Disadvantages

1. Design and production costs are very high, which means that integral construction is used only for mass-produced vehicles.
2. Box-like shape tends to amplify road and engine noise for the occupants. Special sound-deadening materials are used to minimize the transmission of noise.
3. Repairing is difficult.

VARIOUS PANELS IN CAR BODIES

The main panels and parts of the car body are:

- **Bonnet** is the metal cover over the engine compartment. It is also referred to as hood.
- Curved **windscreen**, made of safety glass, gives driver a good field of vision.
- **Windscreen pillar** provides support for windscreen glass.
- **Roof panel** is the simplest and largest of major body panels. Most roof panels have stiffeners consisting of small metal strips placed crosswise to the roof at intervals along the inside surface. These stiffeners welded in place and provide the necessary tacking strips for securing the headlining and inside trim in place.
- **Floor panels** ribbed for stiffness. This panel is composed of several smaller panels welded together to form a single floor unit.
- **Body sill** is usually a major strength member of the structure. This panel is found directly below the bottom of the doors. Body sill supports the floor panel and may be used to combine floor and body.

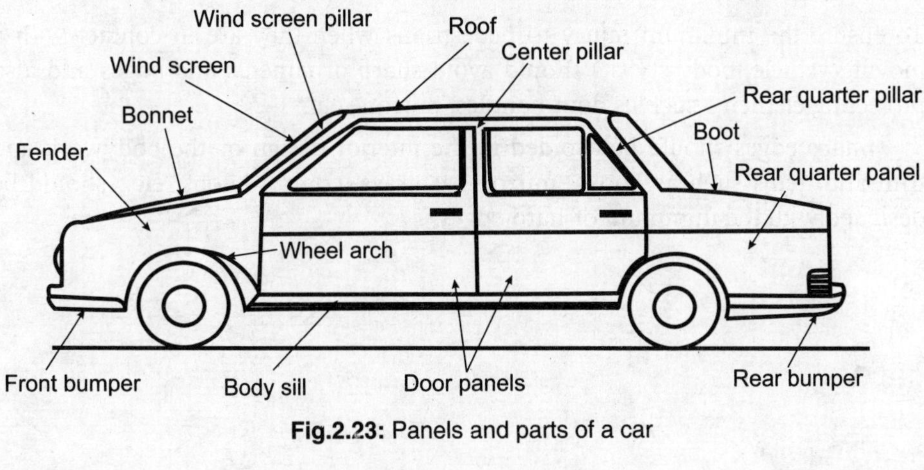

Fig.2.23: Panels and parts of a car

- **Center pillar** is the center vertical support of a four-door saloon, sometimes referred to as B-C port.
- **Rear quarter panel** is the panel between a rear door and the boot and wraps around the wheel well.
- **Fender** is the front quarter panel between the front door and the bonnet. Quarter panels are usually made of sheet metal, but are sometimes made of fiberglass or fiber-reinforced plastic.
- **Boot** is a compartment which accommodates luggage and also spare wheel. **Boot lid** is the metal cover over the luggage compartment. It is also referred to as trunk lid.
- **Doors** strong enough to resist some side impact. The door is composed of outer and inner panels, both being of alloy steel. The door derives most of its strength from the inner panel, since this is constructed mainly to act as a frame for the door. The upper portion of the door has a large opening which can be closed by glass.
- **Bumpers,** a horizontal bar fixed across the front or back of a vehicle to reduce serious damage in a collision or as a trim.
- **Wheel arch** assembly is sometimes constructed as an integral part of the inner construction of the quarter panel (front and rear). It is usually a two piece construction comprising the wheel arch and quarter panel, which are either welded or bolted together.

SAFETY ASPECT OF CAR BODY DESIGN

The designer should ensure the maximum safety of the driver, the passengers and other road users. The vehicle should be designed to reduce the effects of collisions, using such means as careful design of the over-all shape, the selection of suitable materials and the design of components.

SHAPE OF THE VEHICLE

To ensure the minimum injury to pedestrians when they are in contact with a moving vehicle, body stylists should avoid sharp ornaments and edges and also projecting elements such as door handles, mirrors, etc.

Sharp edges should be avoided in the interior design of the bodywork and trim and items such as hooks, mirrors, ashtrays, control knobs, etc., should be designed with the minimum of hard edges.

DESIGN OF THE BODY FOR SAFETY

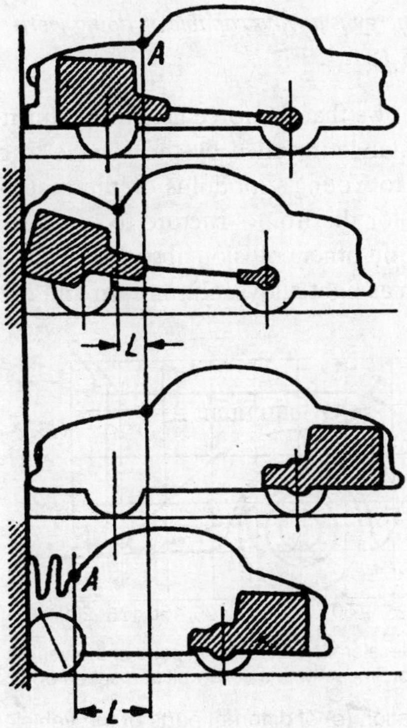

Fig.2.24: Influence of a car on the distance travelled while coming to rest.

To modify the design of a vehicle for optimum characteristics during accidents, the basic energy relation should be considered.

The kinetic energy of a vehicle destroyed during a collision is expressed as:

$$E = (m - \Delta m)v^2/2$$

Where,

m = Total mass of the vehicle

Δm = Moveable mass in the vehicle (passengers and luggage)

v = Velocity

Energy is absorbed by work done on the materials of the vehicle by elastic deformation-strain energy i.e., energy stored in the body due to deformation and this relation can be written as:

$$(m - \Delta m)v^2/2 = (\sigma^2/2E)\,A\,\ell$$

Where,

σ = Local stress in the material

E = Young's modulus

$A\ell$ = Volume of the body

A = Cross-sectional area of the structural material

ℓ = Deformation

Note: *The energy which is absorbed in a body, when strained within elastic limit is known as strain energy. Strain energy is always capable of doing work.*

Strain Energy = Work Done

This expression shows that the force generated during a collision is inversely proportional to the distance travelled by the vehicle in coming to rest and also inversely proportional to Young's modulus of the material. Rear engine vehicle has a greater distance for the front structure to crumple (Fig.2.24). This would indicate that bumpers and other collision absorbing parts of the vehicle should be made of materials such as light alloys, aluminium and rubber.

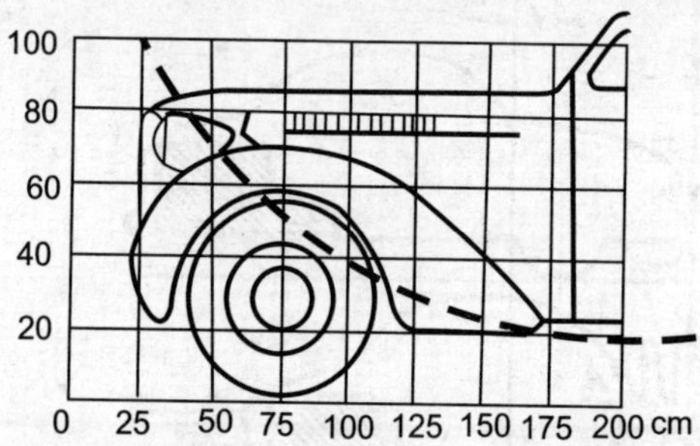

Graph of deceleration of different parts of the vehicle in units of g on impact with a solid wall at a speed of v= 40 km/hr

Fig.2.25: Deceleration (g) of different parts of the vehicles on impact with a solid wall at a speed of V=40 km/hr

Decelerations measured in the passenger compartment of a normal car are usually large, even though only 20% of the maximum retardation is felt in the passenger compartment as seen in Fig.2.25. This is 20g, which is 40 times more than the deceleration experienced during normal braking, although emergency braking may involve retardation up to 1 g.

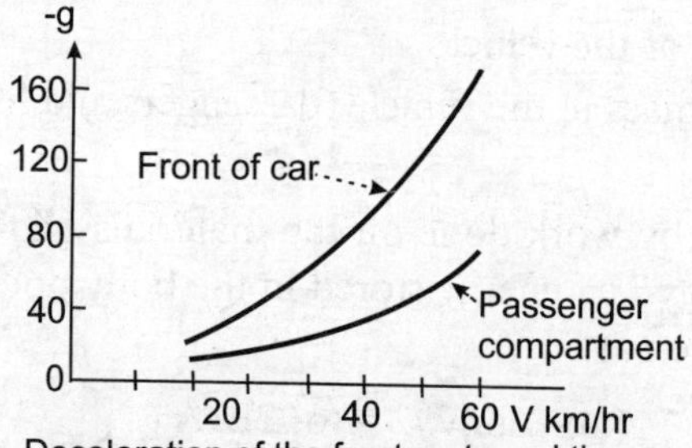

Deceleration of the front parts and the passenger compartment of a passenger car on impact with a solid obstacle

Fig.2.26: Deceleration of front parts and passenger compartment of a car on impact with a solid obstacle.

Fig.2.26 shows the results of experiments to measure the value of retardation at the extreme points of a vehicle and in the passenger compartment.

Long energy absorbing distance

When an accident occurs between two vehicles, decelerations involved are less than when colliding with a solid obstacle. Fig.2.27 shows this relation and clearly indicates the importance of the larger distance over which the force travels before the vehicles come to rest. The graph indicates that long, energy absorbing distances should be provided in vehicle design, and parts of the structure used for this purpose should have lower stiffness than the central section or the passenger compartment of the vehicle.

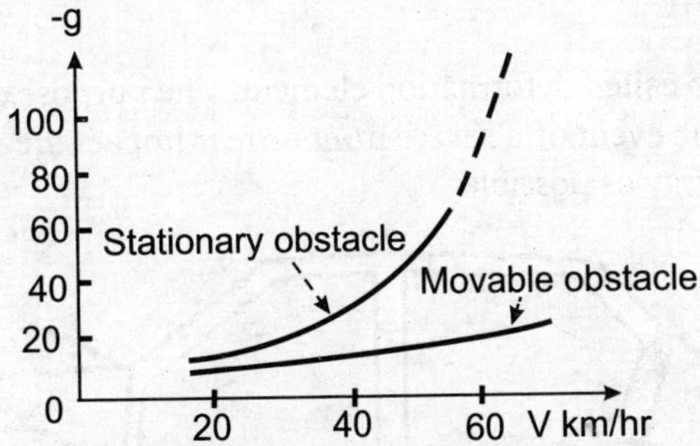

Deceleration of the passenger compartment during a collision with stationary and moving vehicles(second vehicle)

Fig.2.27: Deceleration of passenger compartment during a collision with stationary and moving vehicles (second vehicle)

Rounded bumpers

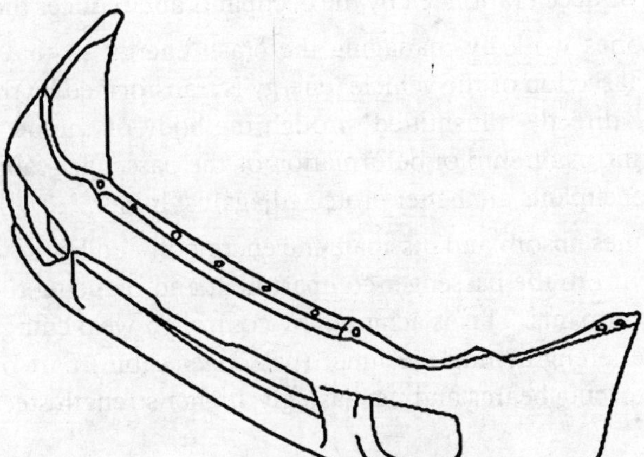

Fig.2.28: Bumper

A bumper is a car shield made of steel, aluminum, rubber, or plastic that is mounted on the front and rear of a passenger car. Bumper beam designed to prevent or reduce physical damage to the front or rear ends of passenger motor vehicles in collision condition. They protect the hood, trunk, grill, fuel, exhaust and cooling system as well as safety related equipment such as parking lights, headlamps and taillights, etc.

A good design of car bumper must provide safety for passengers and should have low weight. The standard specifies the maximum amount of damage a bumper can sustain at speeds up to 10 miles per hour.

Rounded bumpers tend to convert off-centre longitudinal forces into side forces and the vehicle will rotate, reducing the deceleration felt by the occupants.

Crumple zone

Crumple zone is also called deformation element. The purpose of a crumple zone is to ensure that in the event of a severe front or rear impact the vehicle's structure absorbs as much energy as possible.

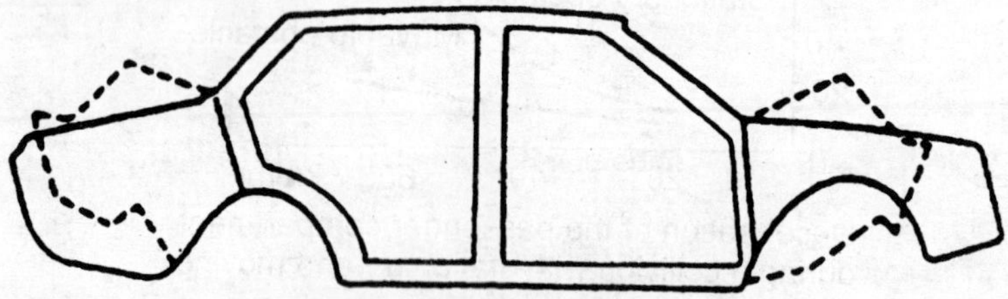

FRONT AND REAR CRUMPLE ZONES ABSORB SHOCK OR IMPACT

Fig.2.29: Crumble zone

Crumple zones is to slow down the collision, not just to absorb energy. This reduces the rate of deceleration felt by the occupants and reduces the risk of injury.

Crumple zones work by managing the crash energy so that it is absorbed within the frontal section of the vehicle (energy is transformed by the deformation instead of being directly transmitted through the body of the occupants), while also preventing intrusion into or deformation of the passenger cabin. This acts to ensure that car occupants are better protected against injury.

Crumple zones absorb and dissipate the energy of a collision, displacing and diverting it away from the passenger compartment and reducing the impact force on the vehicle occupants. This is achieved by controlled weakening of outer parts of the car while strengthening the inner (passenger cabin) part of the body by using more reinforcing beams and increasingly, higher strength steels.

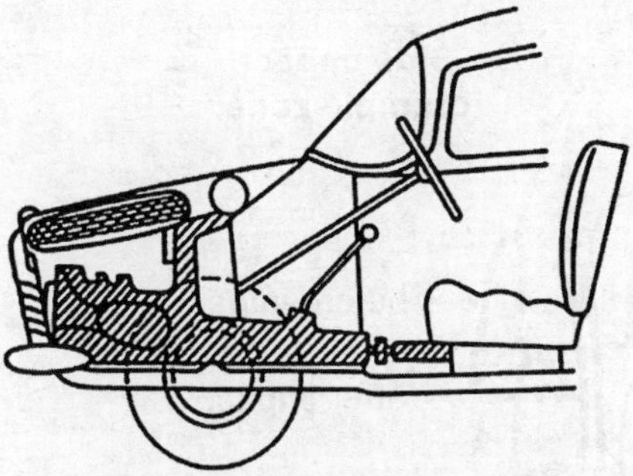

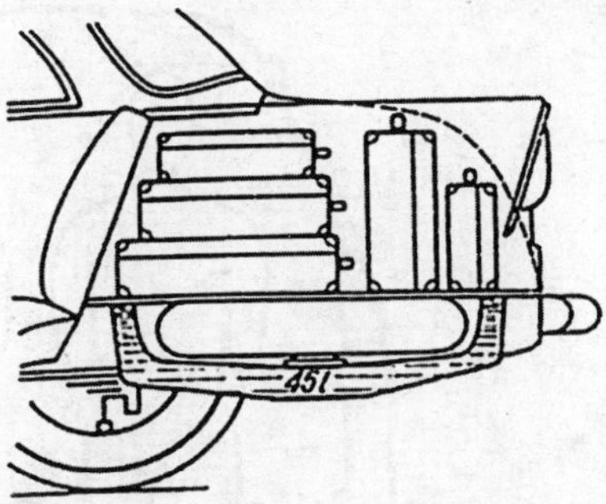

The spare wheel lies in different locations of the vehicle may be part of the crumple zone and if so it must be kept inflated.

Front mounting spare tyre

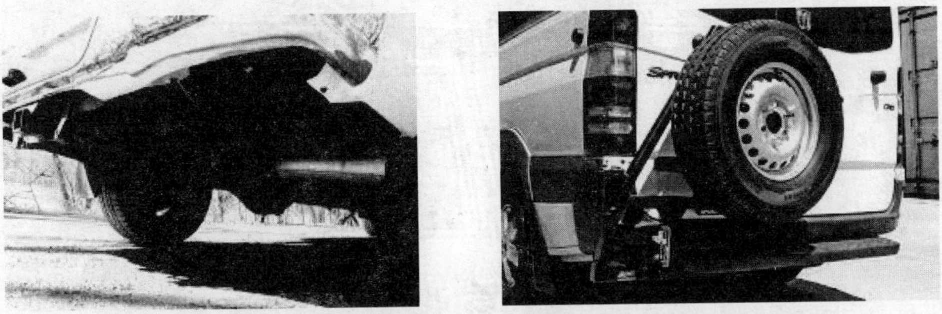

Rear mounting spare tyre

Side mounting spare tyre

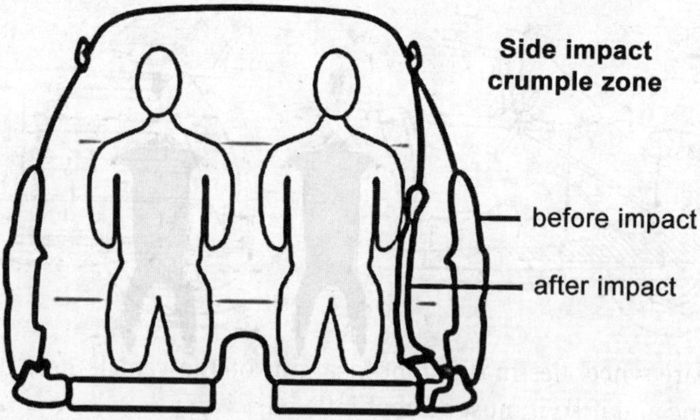

Fig.2.30: Spare tyre as part of crumple zone

The general downside to crumple zones is that repair costs are higher in "fender bender" accidents.

Impact beams

For a side impact, a designer may be able to improve the collision properties of the vehicle by choosing substantial side rails with some elasticity in the lateral direction, especially on buses and commercial vehicles.

To ensure passenger safety during overturning, a stiff roof construction must be used or if this is not possible, local reinforcement or anti-roll bars.

Fig.2.31: Impact beams

One of the most common types comprises strengthening beams fitted into the frame of each door. Side impact beams are metal bars or corrugated panels that bolt or weld inside the door assemblies, as shown in Fig.2.31, to protect the passengers. They prevent the door from opening upon impact and help protect the passenger area.

SAFETY EQUIPMENTS FOR CAR

An important design feature of any modern vehicle is its ability to protect the occupants from serious physical harm resulting from a collision. The response time of a human being does not allow driver and passengers to prepare for an impact of this duration and this indicates that safety devices must be used. All vehicles are now required to pass certain technical safety standards.

Major factors in accidents include driving under the influence of alcohol or other drugs; inattentive driving; crash compatibility between vehicles; driving while fatigued or unconscious; encounters with road hazards such as snow, potholes, and crossing animals; or reckless driving. While human error still plays a big part in causing road accidents, technologies such as anti-lock braking systems, structure-borne sound airbags and innovative ideas, such as airbags on the outside, do promise a safer ride.

The terms "active" and "passive" are used in the context of automobile safety. Active safety devices and systems are those which the vehicle occupant must act to make functional, as for example by fastening a seat belt. Passive safety devices and systems are those, such as air bags, which operate without any input or action from the vehicle occupant.

The following important active and passive safety systems are employed in the modern vehicles.

ACTIVE SAFETY (PRIMARY SAFETY) DEVICES

- Accident avoidance - Preventive measures to reduce the possibility of crashes
- Devices and systems that help keep a car under control and prevent an accident.
- Vehicle occupant must act to make functional

Examples

- Brakes
- Steering
- Seat belts
- ABS
- Traction control
- Collision warning/avoidance
- Adaptive cruise control
- Electronic stability control

SEAT BELT

Seatbelts limit the forward motion of an occupant, stretch to slow down the occupant's deceleration in a crash, and prevent occupants being ejected from the vehicle.

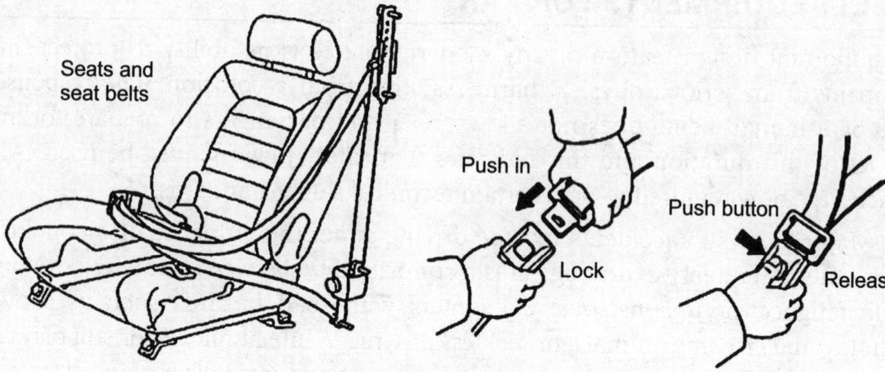

Fig.2.32: Seatbelt

It is essential to have such an automatic device to restrain the body, because in a collision the time to act is too short-one tenth of a second-and the forces are too great to resist. In a really severe crash a human baby effectively weighs the same as a baby elephant.

Operation

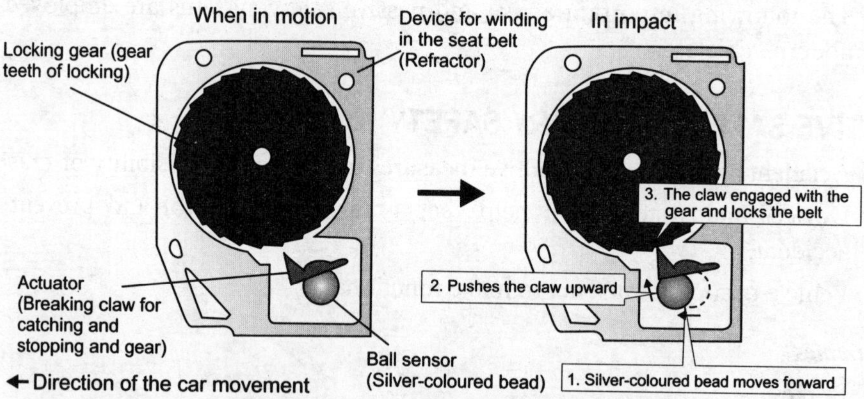

Fig.2.33: Spring loaded inertia mechanism

A seat-belt is made of a woven fabric usually mounted on a spring-loaded inertia mechanism. Under normal driving conditions the seat-belt can be easily pulled off the spool against spring tension. When the vehicle decelerates rapidly as a result of hard braking or impact, a sensor ball is thrown forwards and by means of the actuator plate prevents the spool from unwinding. The seat-belt is now locked in position. When the vehicle comes to rest the ball falls back and the seat-belt is released.

ANTI-LOCK BRAKING SYSTEM

An **ABS** (anti-lock braking system) is a type of an active safety system that helps a driver to avoid skids during panic stops. It is also known as the anti-skid braking system. This system comes into action when the driver suddenly applies brakes during an emergency or on slippery surfaces. Employing antilock braking system on cars and bikes is now mandatory in most parts of the world.

Need for ABS

In a car with a normal braking system, all four wheels will lock and cause the car to skid if the driver suddenly applies brakes in a panic situation. An anti-lock braking system lets a **computer** monitor the wheels. The ABS controls the hydraulic pressure acting on the wheel cylinders to prevent the wheels from locking up. If one of them locks, the computer can **pulse** the brake on that wheel so that the wheel keeps spinning. Because the wheels continue to spin, the driver can continue to control the car with the steering wheel.

Components and operation

The heart of the ABS system is an electronic control unit (ECU) which is provided with inputs from sensors and gives outputs to the controls. The sensors are located at each wheel and send pulse generated signals to the ECU. They indicate whether each wheel is revolving and how fast it is turning.

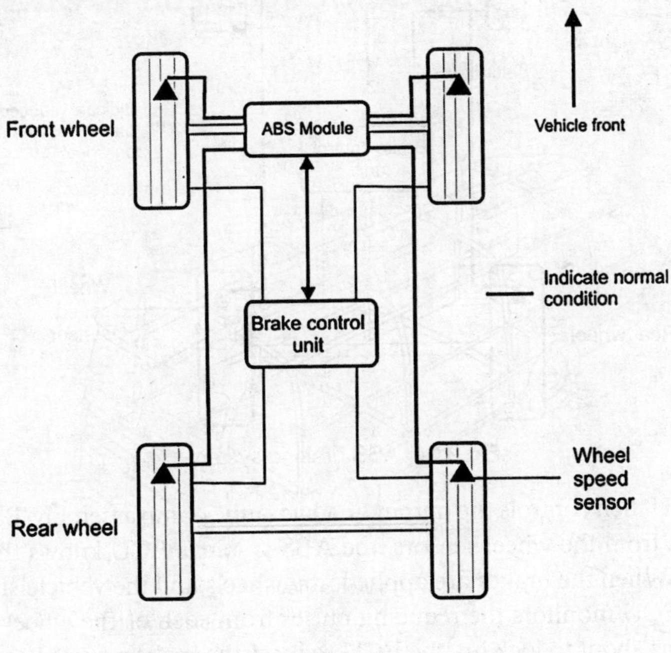

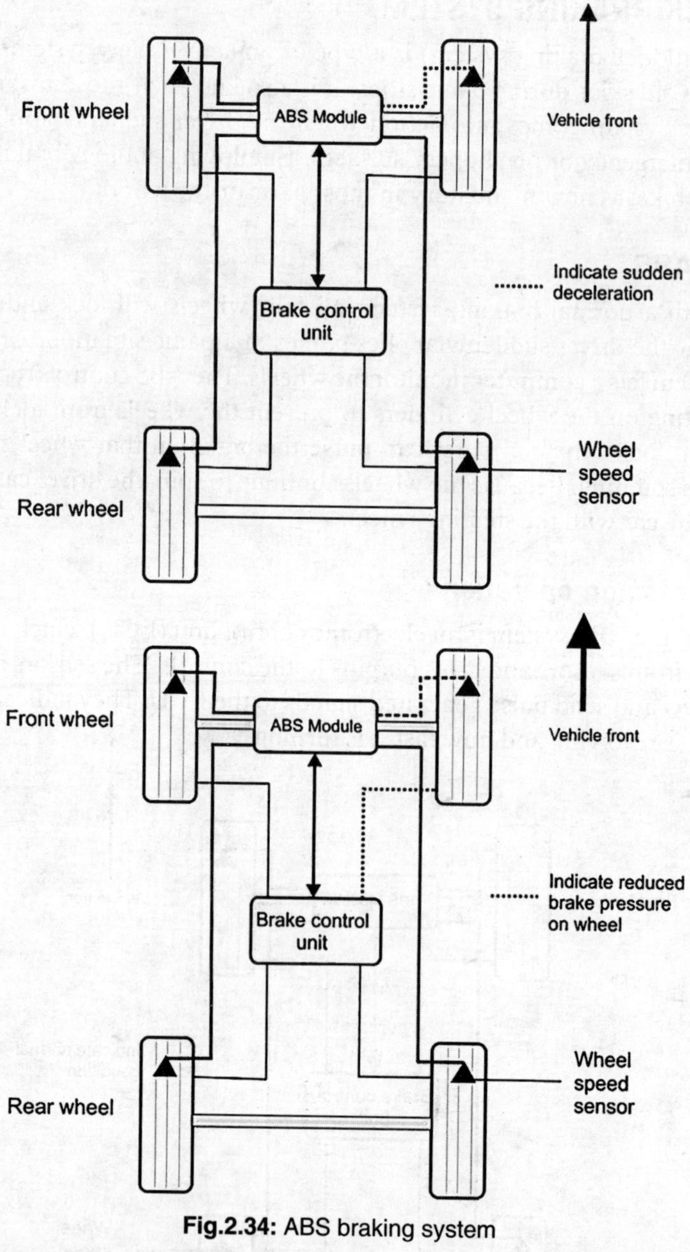

Fig.2.34: ABS braking system

The ECU then controls the output of a hydraulic pump assembly. Based on the input signals from the wheel sensors, the ABS system's ECU knows the speed of each wheel. When the brakes are applied, the wheels and the vehicle start to slow down. The ECU monitors the reducing pulses from each of the wheel sensors. If a wheel seems about to lock up, the ECU reduces the brake pressure at that wheel until the tyre grips again.

Advantages

1. ABS maintains vehicle steerability and stability during panic braking.
2. It reduces braking distance by up to 10% or more especially on wet surfaces.

Disadvantages

The only disadvantage of ABS is its higher cost.

Applications

All high end models of motorcycles, passenger cars, buses and trucks.

TRACTION CONTROL SYSTEM

Traction control systems which restore traction if driven wheels begin to spin.

Traction control system (TCS) optimises grip and stability of the car on the road during acceleration by measuring wheel rotation. It stops wheel spin by reducing engine power or temporarily applying the brakes to that wheel, allowing the car to accelerate smoothly, even on slippery surfaces.

Need for TCS

On roads with a low coefficient of friction, such as snowy, icy or wet roads, the drive wheels spin if the vehicle is started or accelerated quickly, resulting in loss of torque and possibly causing vehicle skidding.

Maintaining the torque at a level appropriate to the coefficient of friction at such times is sometimes difficult for the driver. The traction control system lowers the engine's torque, regardless of the driver's intentions, when the wheels start to spin, while at the same time controlling the brake system, thereby reducing the torque transmitted to the road surface to appropriate levels. In this way, stable and rapid starting and acceleration can be achieved.

WORKING OF TCS

In modern vehicles, traction-control systems utilise the same wheel-speed sensors employed by the antilock braking system. These sensors measure differences in rotational speed to determine if the wheels that are receiving power have lost traction. When the traction-control system determines that one wheel is spinning more quickly than the others, it automatically "pumps" the brake to that wheel to reduce its speed and lessen wheel slip. In most cases, individual wheel braking is enough to control wheel slip. However, some traction-control systems also reduce engine power to the slipping wheels.

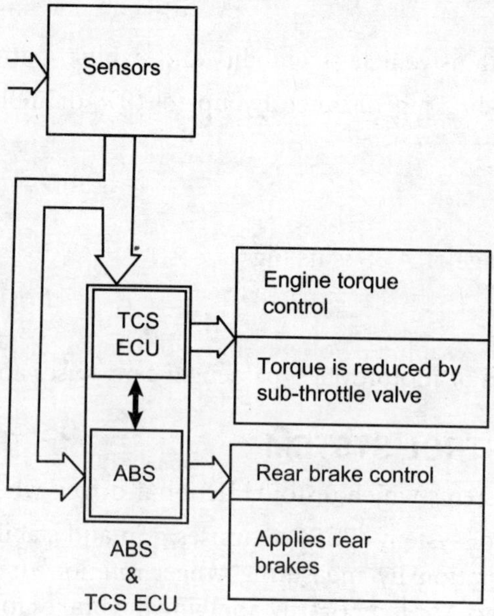

Fig.2.35: Traction control system

Traction control is basically an anti-lock braking system in reverse. Anti-lock brakes prevent the wheels from locking up when the car is decelerating. Traction control keeps the wheels from locking up or skidding when the car is accelerating.

VEHICLE CRUISE CONTROL

Cruise control

Cruise control is employed to retain a steady speed under varying load conditions and relieves the driver from constant foot throttle manipulation. The system is a servomechanism that takes over the throttle of the car to maintain a steady speed as set by the driver.

The constant rate of speed saves some fuel and lessens driver fatigue and leg discomfort (numb problems with aged drivers) during long trips. The key input signals for this system are vehicle speed signal, throttle position signal, and engine speed signal.

Cruise control on wet roads

Cruise control should not be used on wet or icy roads as it can make the vehicle hard to control. When driving in heavy rain or on icy roads with the cruise control set at a safe consistent speed, the wheels begin to hydroplane, the tyres loose traction, and vehicle accelerates to a higher rate of speed. It is roughly estimated car will actually be travelling through the air at 15 to 25 kmph faster than the speed set on the cruise control.

Also when driving in heavy rain or slush conditions with the cruise control set at a desired speed, that one front wheel will hydroplane while the other wheel suddenly gets traction, the car spins out and into the ditch or into traffic.

Adaptive cruise control

Adaptive cruise control (ACC) is a cruise control system in some modern vehicles which maintains a safe distance from the vehicle in front in the same lane.

The system also called active cruise control (ACC) or intelligent cruise control (ICC). This system uses either a radar or laser setup to monitor the distance between the vehicle and the vehicles ahead, and regulates speed. The ACC system decelerates vehicle when necessary to maintain a safe distance between vehicles. When the way is clear, the ACC system resumes preset cruising speed.

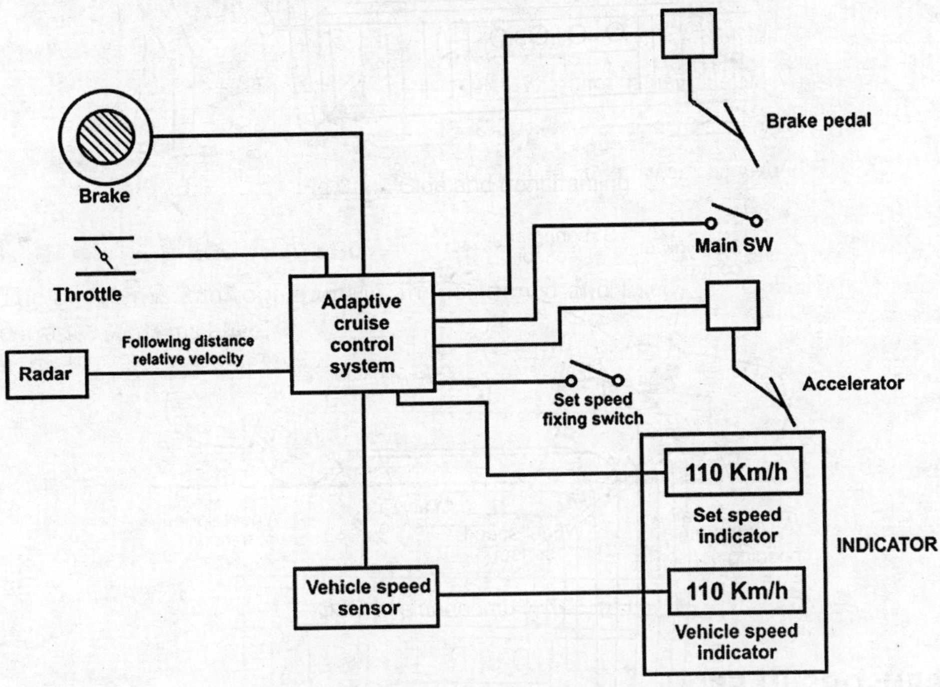

Fig.2.36: Adaptive cruise control system

Although ACC systems automatically take action to control the vehicle's speed, they may not sufficiently decelerate the vehicle in all circumstances to avoid a crash. Depending on the vehicle load, road grade, and vehicle performance parameters, the level of deceleration control typically used by the system is limited to a range between 0.1 and 0.2 g, where g is a unit of force equal to the force exerted by gravity. As a result, drivers remain responsible for the safe operation of their vehicles, and they should use steering and apply the service brakes to avoid a crash.

ELECTRONIC STABILITY CONTROL

Electronic Stability Control (ESC) helps drivers to avoid crashes by reducing the danger of skidding, or losing control as a result of sudden directional change, understeer or oversteer during turns on slippery roads, or hydroplaning. ESC becomes active when a driver loses control of their car. It incorporates the functions of anti-lock braking systems and traction control.

Different manufacturers use different names for their electronic stability control systems. Here are a few:

Other names of ESC	User
Electronic Stability Program (ESP)	Hyundai
Vehicle Stability Assist (VSA)	Honda
Vehicle Stability Control (VSC)	Toyota
Vehicle Dynamic Control (VDC)	Nissan
Dynamic Stability Control (DSC)	BMW
AdvanceTrac with Roll Stability Control	Ford

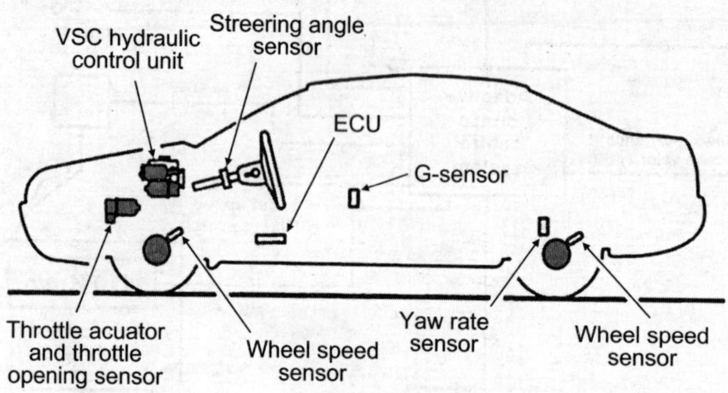

Fig.2.37: Components of ESC

SENSORS IN ESC

ESC incorporates yaw rate control into the anti-lock braking system (ABS). Yaw is rotation around the vertical axis i.e. spinning left or right. Anti-lock brakes enable ESC to brake individual wheels. Many ESC systems also incorporate a traction control system, which senses drive-wheel slip under acceleration and individually brakes the slipping wheel or wheels and/or reduces excess engine power until control is regained. However, ESC achieves a different purpose than ABS or traction control.

The ESC system uses several sensors to determine the driver intention. Other sensors indicate the actual state of the vehicle (response). The most important sensors are:

Steering wheel angle sensor

Steering wheel angle sensor determines the driver's intended rotation; i.e. where the driver wants to steer.

Yaw rate sensor

This sensor measures the rotation rate of the car i.e. how much the car is actually turning. The data from the yaw sensor is compared with the data from the steering wheel angle sensor to determine regulating action.

Lateral acceleration sensor

Lateral acceleration sensor often based on the Hall effect. Measures the lateral acceleration of the vehicle.

Wheel speed sensor

It measures the wheel speed.

WORKING OF ESC

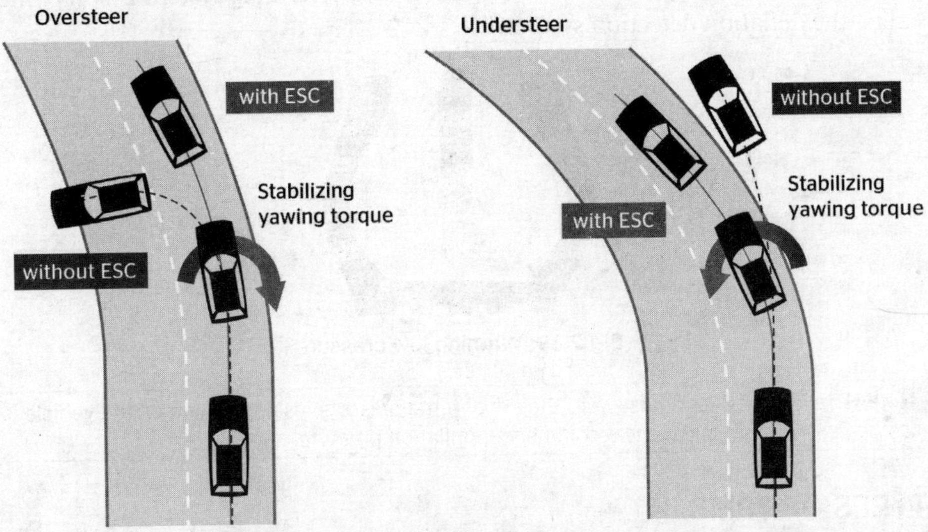

Fig.2.38: Understeer and Oversteer without ESC

During normal driving, ESC continuously monitoring steering and vehicle direction using sensors to determine which direction the driver wants the car to go, and compares that to which way the car is actually going. If the system senses that a skid is imminent or has already started or in other words, that the car is not going in the direction the driver is telling it to go and it can apply the brakes on individual wheels to bring the car back under control. Because the system can brake individual wheels, whereas the driver can only brake all four wheels at once, ESC can recover from skids that a human driver cannot.

Additionally, the system may reduce engine power or operate the transmission to slow the vehicle down.

TYRE PRESSURE MONITORING SYSTEMS (OR) DEFLATION DETECTION SYSTEM

Tyre pressure monitors detect when a tyre drops below the designated pressure and alerts the driver.

NEED FOR TPMS

The inflation pressure of the tyres should be checked regularly, but many motorists do not check their tyres. This is the reason why tyre pressure monitor systems are coming into use. Tyres are designed to operate within a certain pressure range. The recommended inflation pressure is designed to give the best combination of ride comfort, load carrying capacity and rolling resistance.

TPMS refers to the use of a pressure sensor directly mounted on the wheels or tyres of a vehicle. The pressure inside the tyre is measured using a pressure transducer with the pressure information being subsequently sent to the vehicle to warn the driver of under or over inflation of a tyre. This system is sometimes called the deflation detection system.

Fig.2.39: Warning low pressure

Note: The TPMS system must warn the driver if the pressure inside any tyre on the vehicle is 25 percent or more under the recommended inflation pressure.

TYPES OF TPMS

There are essentially two basic ways to monitor tyre pressure electronically: direct method and indirect method.

Direct method

In direct method, a small pressure sensor is located inside each wheel. The sensor has a built-in transponder that broadcasts a radio signal to an external module. The module identifies the signal from each wheel and keeps an eye on pressure. If pressure drops below a predetermined threshold, the module turns on a light or displays a message to warn the driver.

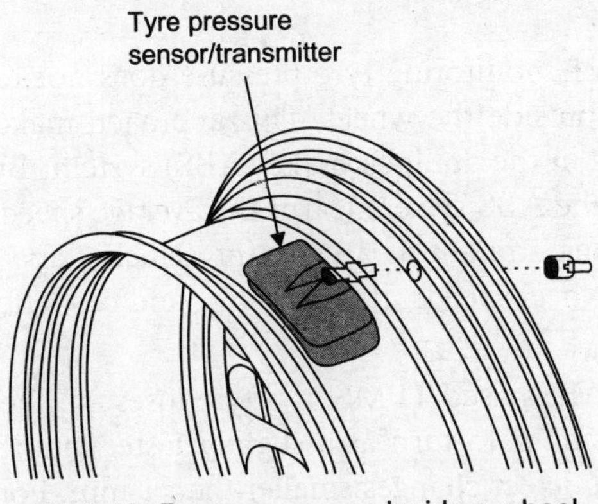

Fig.2.40: Pressure sensor inside a wheel

In direct method, a small pressure sensor is located inside each wheel. The sensor has a built-in transponder that broadcasts a radio signal to an external module. The module identifies the signal from each wheel and keeps an eye on pressure. If pressure drops below a predetermined threshold, the module turns on a light or displays a message to warn the driver.

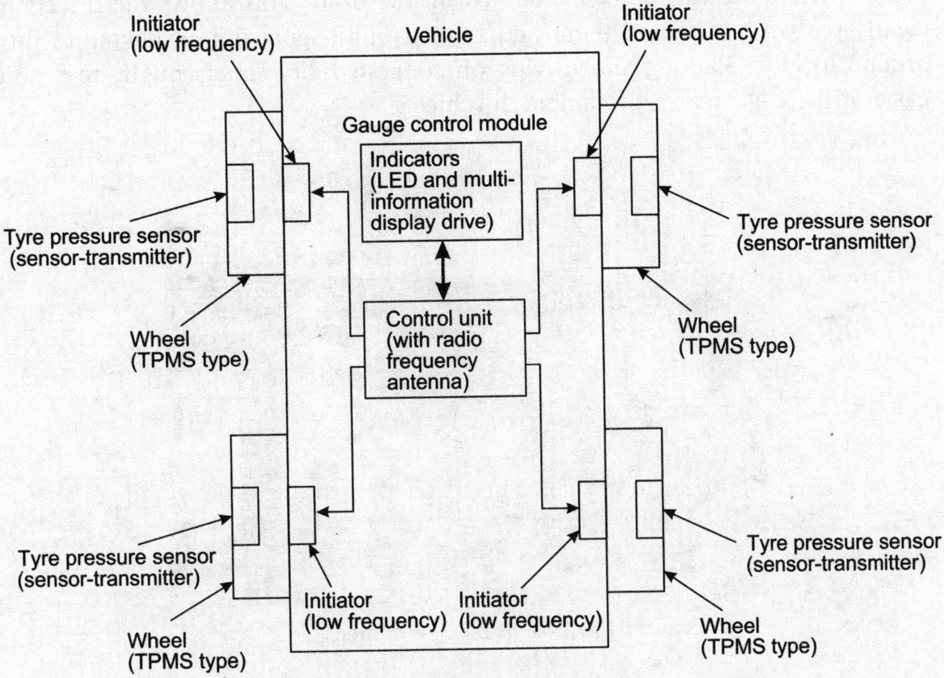

Fig.2.41: Direct type TPMS

The pressure sensors are very accurate but they have their own limitations. One is battery life. The pressure sensor inside each wheel contains a small battery to power the sensor and transponder. Most are long-life lithium batteries that may last from 5 to 10 years.

Indirect method

The other method of monitoring tyre pressure does not require any additional hardware inside or outside the wheel. This approach makes use of the existing wheel speed sensors in the antilock brake (ABS) system. By modifying the ABS operating software, the ABS system learns the average speed at which each wheel rotates when traveling straight at a constant velocity, and detects low tyres by comparing relative wheel speeds. It is a simple, and cost-effective way to monitor tyre pressure.

In the indirect ABS-based TPMS, if a tyre loses air, the diameter of the tyre shrinks slightly causing it to turn at a slightly faster rate than the others. Most ABS systems cannot detect changes smaller than 1 mm. For this reason, indirect ABS-based tyre pressure monitoring systems are not as sensitive as direct TPMS systems that have a pressure sensor inside each wheel.

REAR-VIEW CAMERA

Rear-view camera, also known as reversing camera or backup camera, is a small, wide-angle CCTV (closed circuit TV) camera that is mounted on the rear of the vehicle with a viewing screen mounted on the dash. This allows the drivers to clearly see what is behind them and in their blind spot without having to turn around to look. Parking and driving on congested city streets might be a little easier if there is a rear view camera in vehicles.

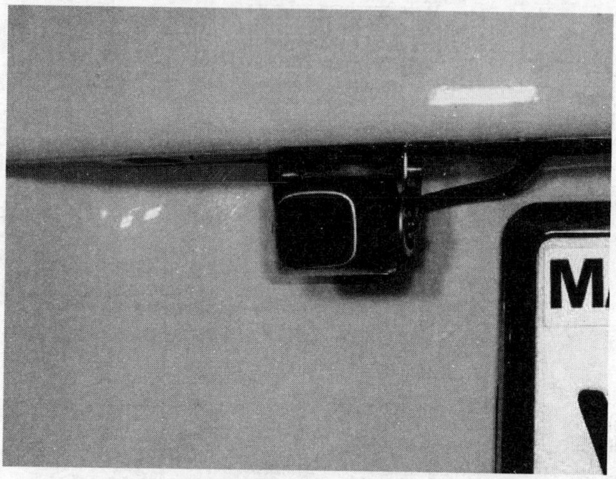

Fig.2.42: Rear view camera

Working of a rear-view camera

The structure of a rear-view camera is different from other cameras. The reflection of a rear-view camera is horizontally flipped so that it produces a mirrored image. This is essential because the driver and the rear-view camera are in opposite positions. The mirrored image is also necessary because it causes the direction of the display to be constant with the mirrors mounted on the motor vehicle. The rear-view camera display is usually wired to automatically sense when the gearbox is set in reverse, and it shows the rear view while the car is in reverse. The other items in the rear of the vehicle are also shown at all times. The rear-view camera usually consists of a wide-angle or fish-eye lens. Although the lens doesn't allow the camera to view distant objects, it does permit the camera to view a continuous horizontal view from one corner, behind the car, to another.

Rear-view cameras are also generally mounted at a downward angle. This allows the camera to show potential barriers on the ground in addition to the location and position of walls and docks that may be looming around the corner.

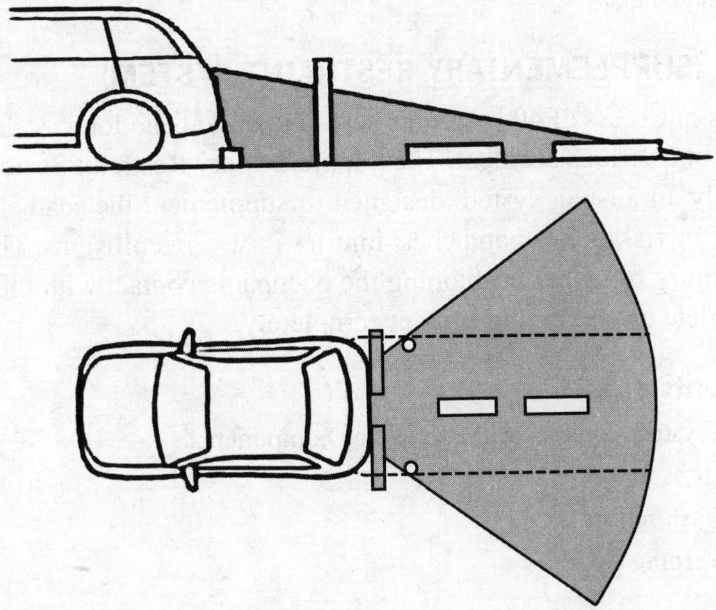

Fig.2.43: Range of view

Benefits

The benefits of rear-view cameras in vehicles are:

1. Eliminate blind zone
2. Keep kids and pets safe
3. Parking
4. Traffic

PASSIVE SAFETY (SECONDARY SAFETY) DEVICES

- Mitigation of injuries - All measures that are taken to reduce injuries during and after accident.

- Operate without any input or action from the vehicle occupant.
- Reactive measures to reduce severity of injuries.

Examples

- Airbags
- Pretensioners in seat belts
- Strong body structure
- Automatic height-adjusted headrests
- Warning devices (light or voice)
- Crumple zone
- Laminated glass

AIRBAG (SUPPLEMENTARY RESTRAINT SYSTEM)

At speeds in excess of 40 kmph the seat belt alone is no longer adequate in the event of a serious accident. The Supplementary Restraint System (SRS) is basically an air-bag system designed to supplement the seatbelt system to reduce the risk of head and chest injuries in severe collisions. The airbag reduces injury by either cushioning the occupants contact with the interior of the vehicle or preventing contact completely.

Components of SRS

An air bag system consists of the following components.

1. Air bag module
2. Crash sensor
3. Warning lamp

NOTE: The Supplemental Restraint System can function only when the ignition switch is in the II position.

Airbag module

Airbag for the driver is located in the steering wheel center pad. In an impact above 40 km/h, crash sensors send a signal to the electronic control unit (ECU), which triggers the igniter unit. Propellants that create a gas when burnt are then ignited. The air bag is then inflated. As the body of the occupant sinks into the airbag, the gas is forced out of vent holes and the body is cushioned.

The SRS is designed to function on a one time only basis. In the event the SRS deploys, the airbag module will not function again and must be replaced.

An air bag module has three main parts: the air bag, the inflator, and the propellant.

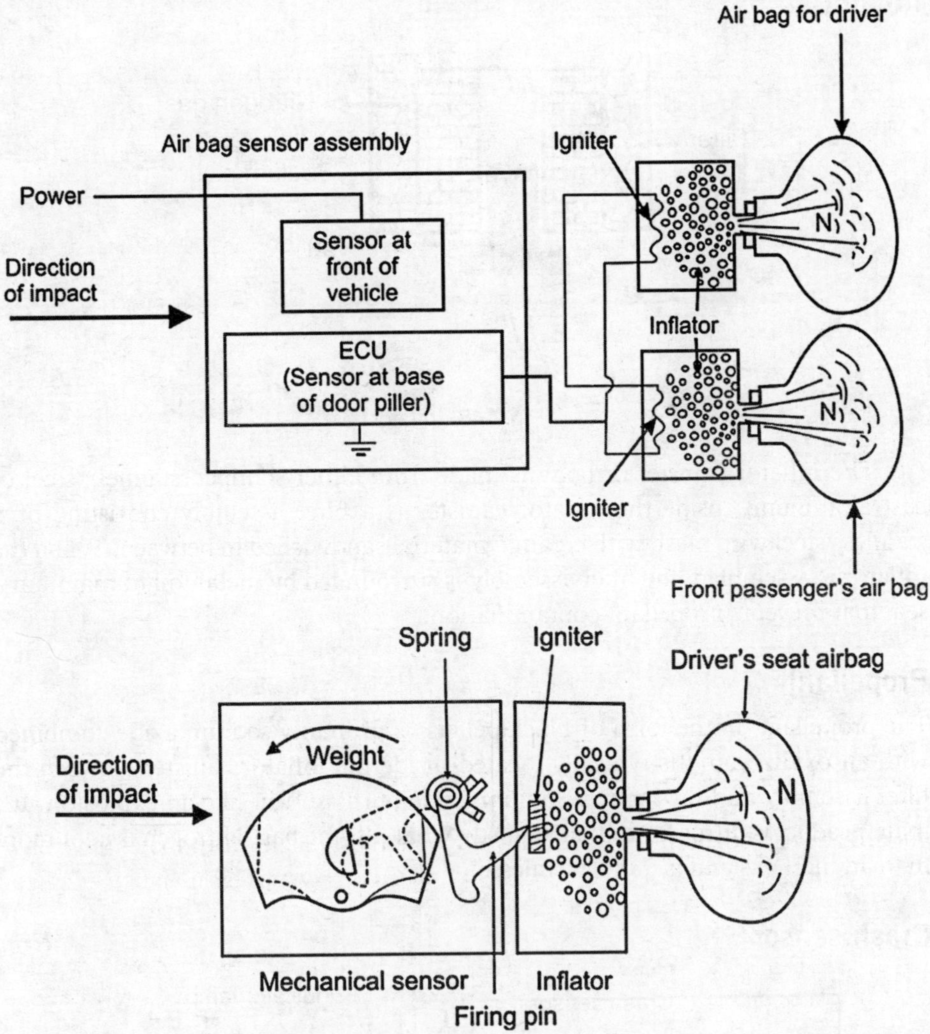

Fig.2.44: Supplementary restraint system

Airbag

The airbag is made from a woven nylon fabric and comes in different shapes and sizes depending on specific vehicle requirements. The driver's-side airbag material is manufactured with a heat shield coating to protect the fabric from scorching, especially near the inflator assembly, during deployment. Talcum powder or corn starch is also used to coat the air bag. These substances prevent the fabric from sticking together and make it easier to assemble. Newer silicone and urethane coated airbag materials require little or no heat shield coating, although talcum powder or corn starch will probably still be used as a processing aid.

Inflator

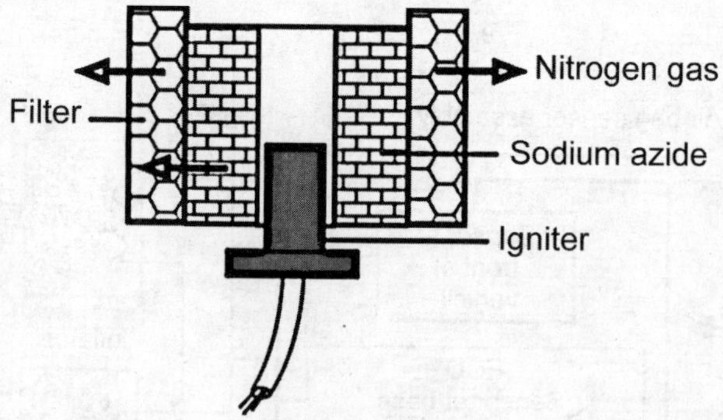

Fig.2.45: Inflator

The inflator canister or body is made from either stamped stainless steel or cast aluminum. Inside the inflator canister is a filter assembly consisting of a stainless steel wire mesh with ceramic material sandwiched in between. When the inflator is assembled, the filter assembly is surrounded by metal foil to maintain a seal that prevents propellant contamination.

Propellant

The propellant, in the form of black pellets, is primarily sodium azide combined with an oxidizer and is typically located inside the inflator canister between the filter assembly and the igniter. Sodium azide burns so fast like an explosion. It's main product is nitrogen, so that's mostly what fills the bag. Nitrogen is a lot more than an inert gas and is quite harmless.

Crash sensor

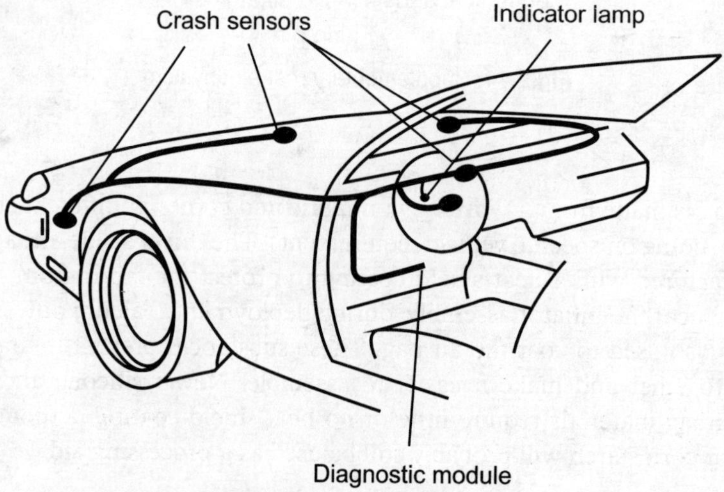

Fig.2.46: Crash sensor

The crash sensors must be able to detect a collision and convert it into corresponding signals within milliseconds. The airbag control unit receives this signal, deploys the airbags and belt tensioners. Additional, remote crash sensors are also located on the vehicle to assist with crash detection.

The measurement principle employed by the crash sensors is usually based on the effect of inertia. When a vehicle is stopped abruptly by an impact, all bodies or objects which are not firmly fixed to the vehicle will continue to move at the impact speed.The sensors' design enables them to measure this acceleration and relay it to the control unit as usable data.

Warning light

When the SRS warning or indicator light is illuminated on the dash, this means that the airbag control unit sees an issue in the system and has disabled the system. This means that the airbags will not deploy in the event of an accident.

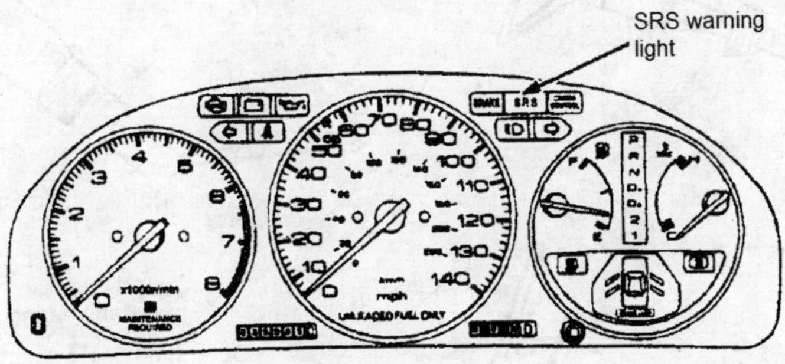

Fig.2.47: SRS warning light

A malfunction is shown by:

1. The indicator light flashing or flickering.
2. The indicator light fails to illuminate when the ignition switch is first turned to the II position.
3. The indicator light continuously illuminated.
4. The indicator light illuminated while driving.

LAMINATED WINDSHIELD

Laminated windshields remain in one piece when impacted, preventing penetration of unbelted occupants' heads and maintaining a minimal but adequate transparency for control of the car immediately following a collision. Tempered glass side and rear windows break into granules with minimally sharp edges, rather than splintering into jagged fragments as ordinary glass does.

COLLAPSIBLE STEERING WHEEL AND COLUMN

Collapsible steering wheels or columns reduce the risk and severity of driver impalement on the column in a frontal crash.

The steering wheel or column can be designed to collapse on impact. In the event of collision, the driver is exposed to the risk of injury from the steering wheel and steering column. The tubular steering column is made of an "expanded-metal" grid so that, although strong in twist, it collapses and absorbs energy if compressed lengthwise (Fig.2.48a).

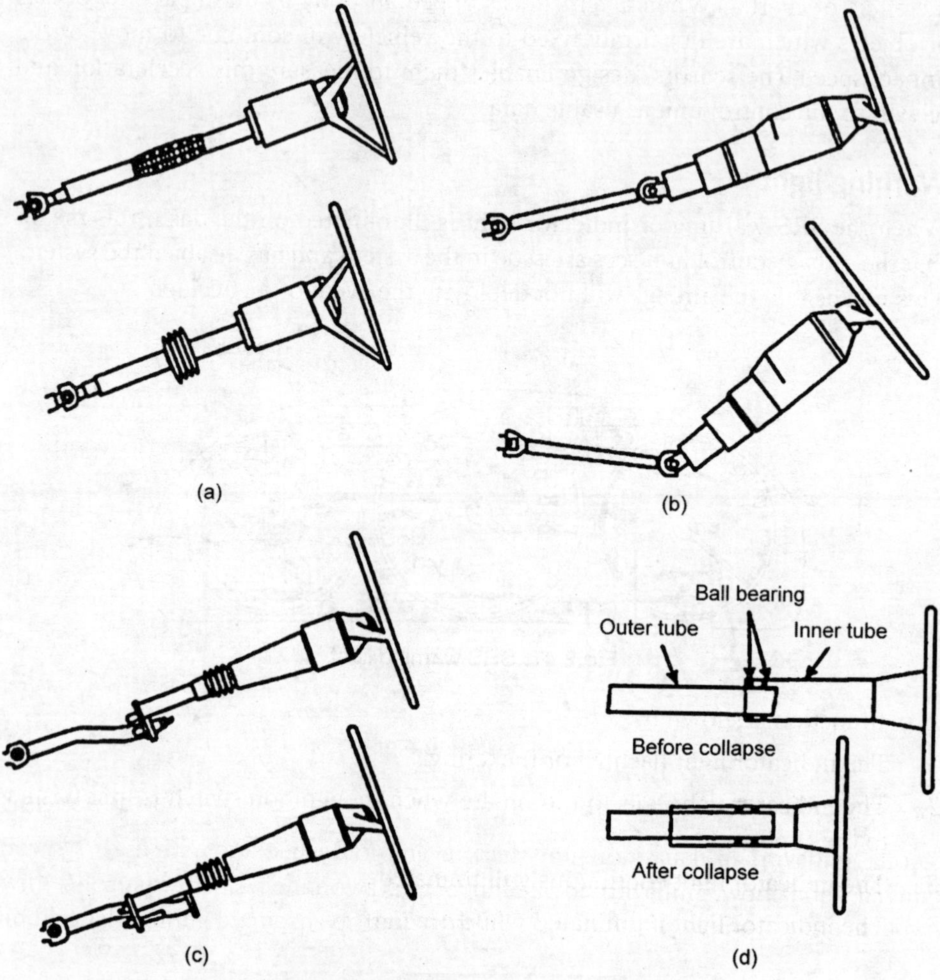

Fig.2.48: Collapsible steering columns

One steering column, which can be angled to suit the driver's needs, collapses at a universal joint on impact (Fig.2.48b). Another design divides the steering shaft into sections which are connected by joints, but not placed in line. During the front-end collision, the lower portion of the column rides up the upper portion to absorb impact energy (Fig.2.48c).

In the other type (Fig.2.48d), the safety steering column has an upper and a lower steering spindle, connected by a tube. The lower spindle is secured in the tube by a ball bearing or a plastic rivet. The outer tube is not a solid, but consists of an expanded metal mesh. In the event of a collision the mesh outer tube deforms, the balls make grooves in the tubes or the plastic rivet is sheared off and the lower spindle is pushed up into the tube. Deformation of the outer tube absorbs the impact force before it can reach the steering wheel and the spindle sliding in the tube avoids the risk of injury.

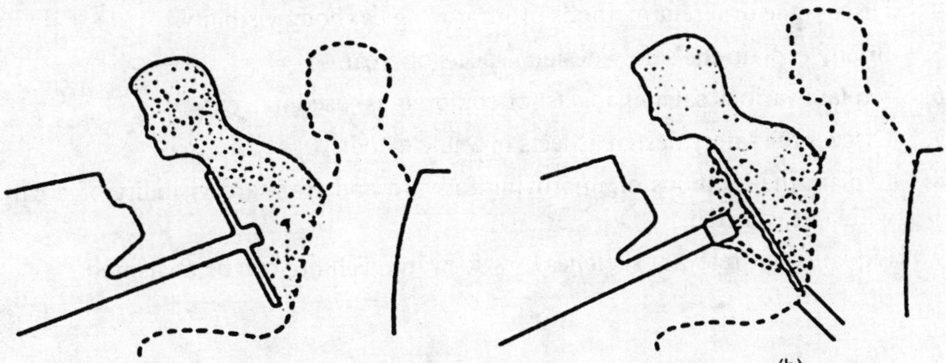

(a) (b)

Fig.2.49: (a) Steering column acts as a spike;
(b) Dished steering whell absorbs impact of a driver

The steering wheel is "dished" and provided with a large boss and wide spokes in order to spread the load of impact over the driver's chest. The wheel or boss can also be designed to collapse when under a pre-determined load.

Review Questions

Short Questions

1. What are the importances of vehicle body design?
2. Write the classification of car bodies.
3. Draw the layout of four door saloon and also specify its salient features.
4. What is meant by limousine?
5. Indicate the salient features of limousine with a neat sketch.
6. Write down the safety design aspects of a car.
7. List out the various panels in car bodies.
8. What is the importance of downward visibility?
9. Indicate the seating dimensions for the driver of a passenger car.
10. How forward visibility can be improved?
11. What is crumble zone in vehicle construction?
12. With a sketch illustrate the features of roof panel.

Long Questions

1. Explain the construction of a passenger car with neat sketches.
2. Explain the classification of passenger cars with sketches.
3. Discuss in detail the visibility regulations in car body.
4. Discuss the different methods of improving car body visibility.
5. Briefly explain the safety design aspects of a car.
6. Explain various safety gadgets (or equipments) used in a car.
7. Discuss the safety design aspects of vehicle body.
8. Explain the methods of improving forward and rearward visibility of a car with a neat sketch.
9. Explain with relevant sketches how forward visibility can be measured.

3 Bus Body Details

Bus body means the portion of a bus that encloses the bus's occupant space, exclusive of the chassis.

TYPES OF BUS BODY

BASED ON CAPACITY

Buses can be classified according to their size and seating capacity.

Low capacity

Low capacity vehicle include:

Micro bus	Max. 12 passengers plus driver
Mini bus	13-22 passengers plus driver

Medium capacity

Medium capacity vehicle include:

Mini bus	23-34 passengers plus driver
Standard bus	35-70 passengers plus driver

High capacity

High capacity vehicles are the vehicles with seating capacity more than 70 passengers plus driver and include vehicles such as:

- Single deck articulated bus
- Single deck double articulated bus
- Double deck bus
- Double deck articulated bus
- Single deck tandem axle bus

BASED ON DISTANCE TRAVELLED

Passenger carrying vehicles are most easily classified by the average distance of their route.

Town buses

Town buses are used for short distance transport up to 20 km. They have a large number of standing places, at least two wide doors with large entry and exit platforms and hard single, double and continuous seats covered with durable plastic materials. They also have side walls, floor and wall pillars of greater thickness than the other types of buses for improved strength.

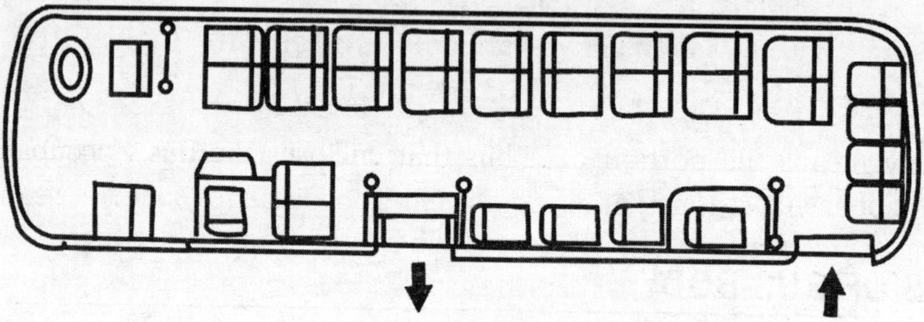

Fig.3.1: Town bus

Suburban buses

Suburban buses are used for distances of about 40 km. They usually have reasonably comfortable double and continuous seats and a fairly small entry platform which can serve as a space for luggage or extra standing passengers. Usually one door is sufficient for this type of operation.

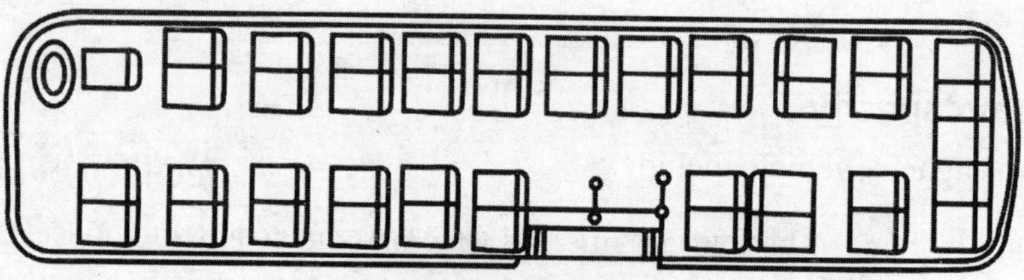

Fig.3.2: Suburban bus

Inter-city coaches

Inter-city coaches are used for long distances of about 200 or more. These coaches have comfortable double and continuous seats with under-floor luggage space and roof racks for large items of luggage.

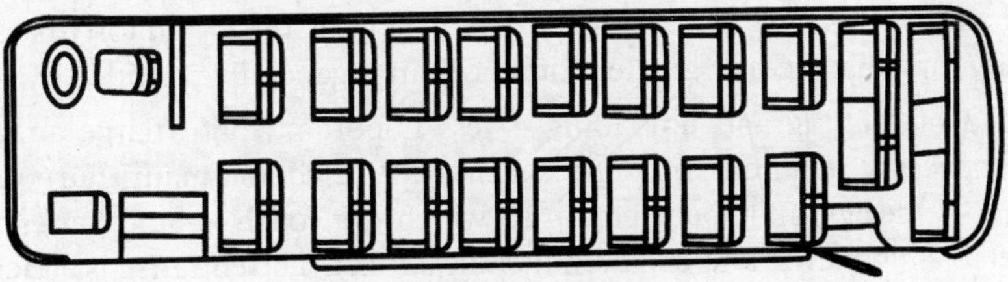

Fig.3.3: Inter-city bus

Sleeper coaches

These vehicles are full-sized coaches, but are only designed internally to carry between 8 and 18 passengers. There are always full galley facilities, comfortable lounges and bunk beds to allow the passengers to eat, relax and sleep during the journey. These vehicles sometimes have blacked out or mirrored windows, allowing passengers to see out, but preventing fans from peering in. They are well equipped, as the comfort of the passengers is paramount. DVD players, large screen TV, and game systems are now the norm, while some vehicles even have personal DVD players and screens in each bunk.

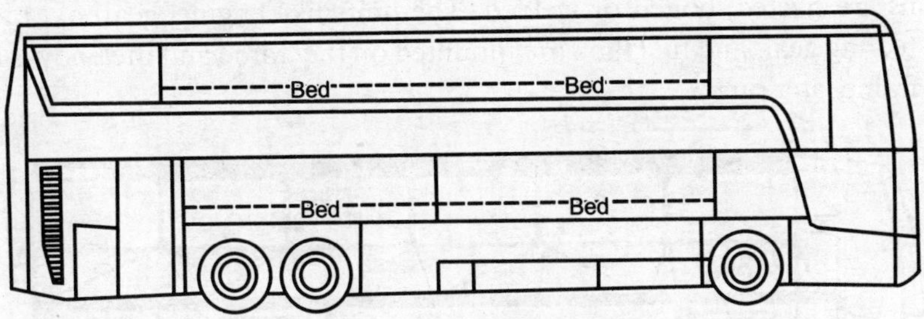

Fig.3.4: AC sleeper coach

Touring coaches

For long distance touring coaches, very comfortable reclining double seats, air-conditioning, music player, rest rooms, etc are provided. Extra transparent windows in the roof are provided for additional visibility for passengers. Thermal and acoustic insulation is usually elaborate and spacious luggage compartments are provided under the floor and on the roof.

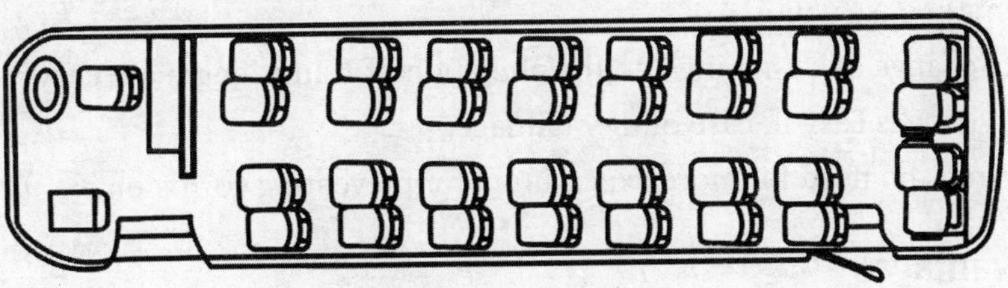

Fig.3.5: Touring coach

Vehicles of this type are designed to carry between thirty and forty passengers over fairly long distances in greater comfort than is generally provided by buses.

Speed of loading and unloading is less important, but a large amount of luggage space is required. Modern coaches are used for many purposes and therefore the design and specification to which the coach is built varies from a low level to a high level, and can even include a toilet. The entrance is either at the front or behind the front wheels.

Some buses and coaches are made with the body structure forming the main frame; although this is not very common it has the advantage of reducing overall weight.

BASED ON CONSTRUCTION

Conventional design

In conventional type, ladder type chassis frame is the main load bearing element. Ladder type frame consists of side and cross members. The side and cross members are connected with special gusset sections or pressed cross member sections. The junctions are riveted, bolted or welded. The units like engine, gearbox, radiator, axles, steering gear, and fuel tank are mounted on the frame and the body is bolted on the frame later on.

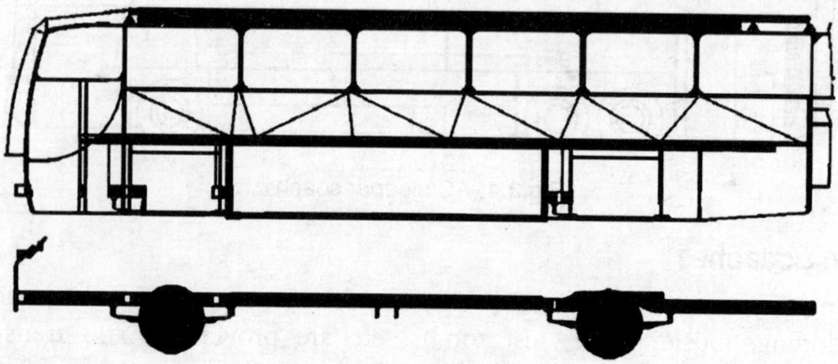

Fig.3.6: Conventional design

Advantages

1. Simple construction
2. The change of designing and the alteration of frame length are easy.
3. Servicing is easy in case of any damage.
4. There is no need for more expenditure for preventing corrosion.

Disadvantages

1. The weight of the frame is more, due to this the vehicle speed is decreased. More fuel is also required.

2. Since the floor height is more, the centre of gravity from the ground will also be more. Due to this, the stability will be decreased.

Integral design

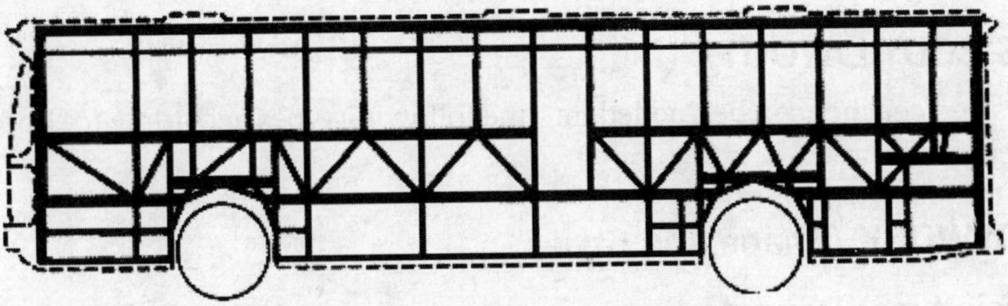

Fig.3.7: Integral bus design

In the integral bus construction, a base structure is formed by building a structure with four long side members, cross members, outriggers and wheel arch supports. Units like engine, gearbox, axles, etc, are mounted on the flexible under-structure which is fabricated by welding.

BASED ON THE COMFORT

Non-Deluxe bus

Non Deluxe Bus (NDX) means bus designed for basic minimum comfort level.

Semi-Deluxe bus

Semi Deluxe Bus (SDX) means a bus designed for a slightly higher comfort level and with provision for ergonomically designed seats.

Deluxe bus

Deluxe Bus (DLX) means a bus designed for a high comfort level and individual seats and adjustable seat backs, improved ventilation and pleasing interiors.

AC-Deluxe bus

A.C. Deluxe Bus (ACX) means a Deluxe Bus which is air conditioned.

BASED ON THE PURPOSE

Buses can also be classified according to their purposes. Some of the special purpose buses are listed below.

- Sleeper Coach
- School Bus
- Tourist Bus

- Prison vehicles
- Ambulances
- Off road vehicles
- Vehicle Designed for use by Police, Security and Armed Forces

BUS BODY LAYOUT

Buses and coaches can be divided into the following types according to: Bodywork and engine location.

BODYWORK (Shape and Style)

Classic type (Bonneted)

The classic or normal control bus has the engine in front of the passenger carrying compartment. This design is disappeared due to its low ratio of useful length to overall length but it also has a high tare weight and poor aerodynamic shape.

Fig.3.8: Classic type (Bonneted)

Single deck bus

The full length bodywork single deck bus or coach is almost universal today as this layout eliminates all the disadvantages with bonneted type.

These vehicles are designed to transport numbers of passengers, up to about forty of whom may be carried on a single floor or deck. Fig.3.9 shows a single decker bus, which has its entrance to the front, where the driver can observe passengers boarding or alighting from the vehicle. The doors are normally power operated by the driver to prevent passengers getting on or off when the bus is moving.

In towns and cities there are usually short distances between stops, and speed of loading and unloading passengers is very important. The entrance to the bus is about 300 mm above ground level, an easy step up from the edge of the pavement. From this platform another step up leads up to the deck of the bus.

To make room for the front entrance and to help reduce the floor height, the engine and transmission are placed at the rear of the vehicle.

Fig.3.9: Single deck bus

Double deck bus

In some cities double deck buses are used. These buses have a greater number of seats for a given overall length, but stability is not as high as for the single decker.

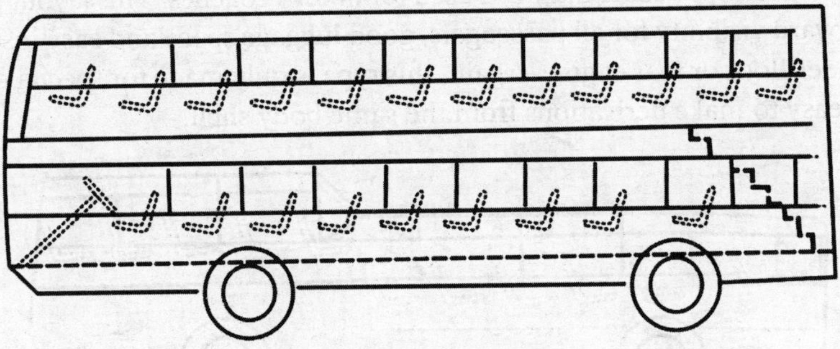

Fig.3.10: Double deck bus

A double-decker bus capable of seating about sixty passengers is shown in Fig.3.10. Construction and Use Regulations stipulate a maximum height for the vehicle and a minimum ceiling height for both upper and lower decks. This means that the floor of the lower deck must be fairly close to the ground; the engine and transmission are once again situated at the rear of the vehicle.

In older designs of double-decker bus the entrance was placed to the rear of the vehicle, the disadvantage of this arrangement is that the driver is unable to see passengers getting on and off except with the aid of mirrors, which do not give an adequate view of people on the platform or those running to catch the bus. By placing the platform at the front the driver can have a direct view of passengers boarding and alighting, as in the case of the single-decker bus shown in Fig.3.9.

Exit doors can be placed in the centre of the bus which permits the entry and exit of the passengers at the same time, allowing a shorter stop to pick up and drop off passengers.

Split-level type

An intermediate solution between the two is the split-level layout having more seats than a single decker and more stability than the double decker. However, owing to the small number of derivations or variations that can be made from this basic design, it has not been widely accepted.

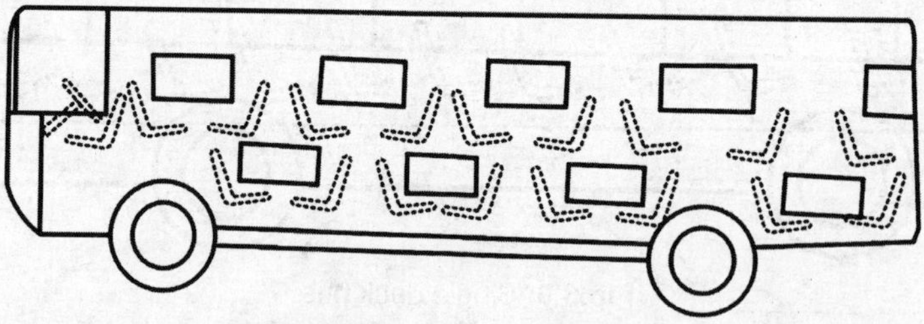

Fig.3.11: Split-level type

Two-level single decker

The two-level single decker has been used for luxury coaches. This layout provides good forward visibility for all passengers, good luggage space and easy installation of an under-floor or rear engine. Again, this type is only made for special orders as it is not easy to make derivations from the same body shell.

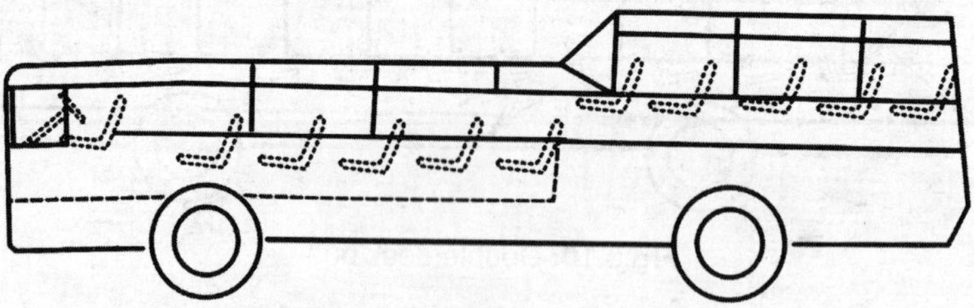

Fig.3.12: Two-level single decker

Articulated

Bodies for very large coaches or in particular, city buses are often made in two parts because of axle load limitations. The rear portion is articulated to the main vehicle by a covered pivot allowing free movement of passengers between them.

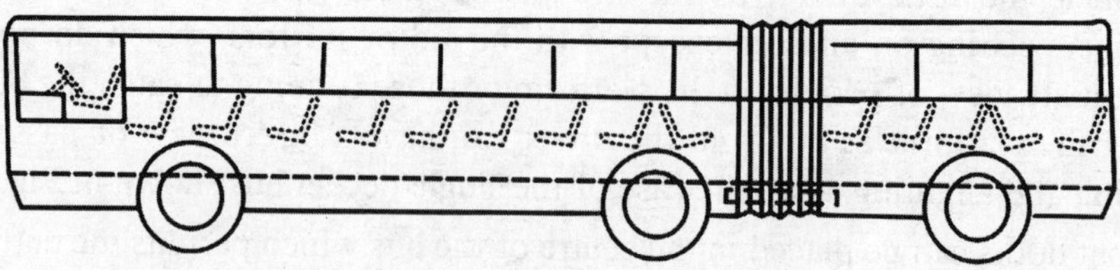

Fig.3.13: Articulated

ENGINE LOCATION

The basic aim when designing a bus or coach body is the best possible utilization of the floor space so that the largest number of passengers can be accommodated with the highest possible level of comfort in a given type of coach or bus.

Fig.3.14 illustrates the influence of engine location to improve the utilization of overall surface area of a commercial vehicle.

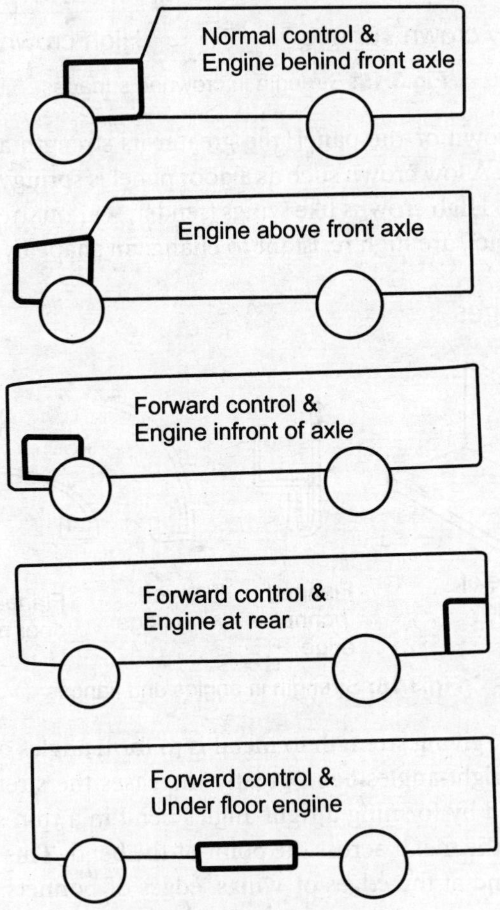

Fig.3.14: Engine location

TYPES OF METAL SECTIONS USED

Crowns

The stress concentration at the bend is an important consideration in the design and manufacture of the car body. The most common features of the body are the curved surfaces. These are called crowns and may be curved either in one direction or in all directions. A crowned surface is stronger than a flat panel while it will resist any force tending to change its shape. It also has the ability to return to its original shape unless distorted beyond its point of elasticity.

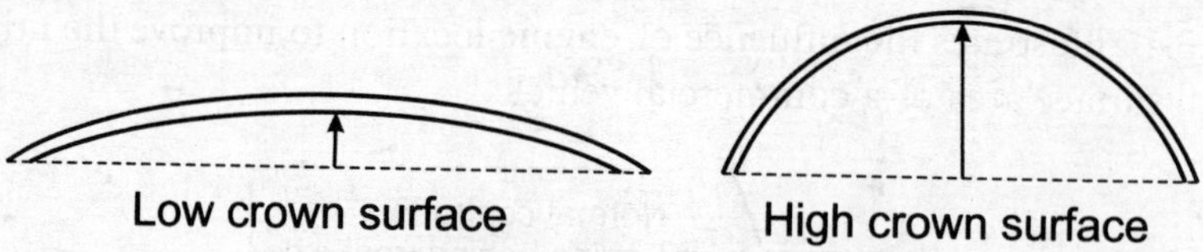

Fig.3.15: Strength in crowned surfaces

The greater crown of the panel, the greater its strength and rigidity to resist change in its shape. A low crown such as a door panel is springy and is low resistant to change of shape. High crowns like wings (fender, rear quarter panels, etc), edges of roof, body sill, etc., are high resistant to change in shape by an outside force.

Angles and flanges

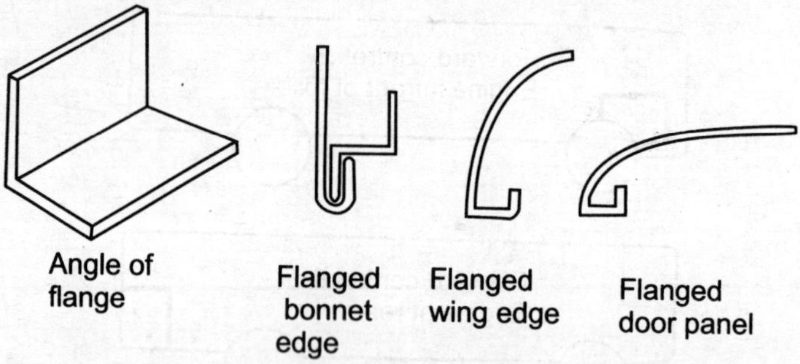

Fig.3.16: Strength in angles and flanges

A further method of giving strength to metal is to form angles or flanges along the edges of sheets. A right-angles bend greatly increases the strength of a sheet, as can be demonstrated by forming a right-angles bend in a thin sheet of metal and then trying to bend the metal across the point of the bend. This method is used on inner door panels and at the edges of wings, edges of bonnets and boot lids, and wherever stiffness is required at unsupported edges.

Sections

Much more strength can be gained by making a U-channel (comprises two right-angled bends) instead of a single-angled bend in any reinforcement section. The U-channel is also the most common type of section used in the construction of car frames.

Another method of increasing strength is known as box construction, which consists of two U-sections welded together to form a square pillar or box.

Box sections are used in conjunction with U-channel construction in the manufacture of car chassis frames, underbodies, subframes, cross members and any construction where great strength is necessary.

Channel section steel pressings of constant web height are usually employed for the chassis frame side-members. Although the use of channel section provides adequate resistance to vertical bending loads, it is much less efficient in resisting sideways bending and torsional (twisting) loads. This type of frame is economical to produce and also provides for easy attachment of the cross-members and the various other mounting brackets.

The cross-members must resist torsional deflection of the frame as a whole.

In order to provide a good resistance to bending and torsional effect, the frame sections are made of proper forms.

Table 3.1: Frame sections and behaviours

Frame Section		Behaviour
Flat		Offers little resistance to bending and twisting.
Channel		Excellent resistance to bending. Resistance increases as depth of section is increased.
Tubular		Excellent resistance to torsion. Resistance increases as diameter is increased.
Box		Good resistance to both bending and torsion.
Top-hat		Not commonly used due to weakness and a propensity to rust.
I		Good resistance to bending and torsion.

Channel section is usually employed for the side members as it provides good resistance to vertical bending loads, but with minimum weight. A further advantage of channel section is that it allows easy attachment of the cross members and mounting of other components. However, channel section provides only a limited resistance to torsion forces (i.e. poor in torsion) and is therefore unsuitable for the construction of cross members. As the cross members must be capable of resisting torsional effects, they may be formed from tubular or circular section, although for convenience a box section is sometimes employed.

Various other material sections may be used for the construction of cross members. These include the top-hat section and the I-section which is manufactured from two channel sections placed back-to-back. Provided the correct material section is used, the chassis frame can be made rigid enough to withstand the loads placed upon it.

REGULATIONS

Buses are categorized into four types:

TYPE I

Type I vehicles are the medium and high capacity vehicles designed and constructed for urban and sub urban / city transport with area for standing passengers, to allow movement of passengers associated with frequent stops and the low capacity vehicles which are designed and constructed for urban and sub urban / city transport exclusively for carrying seated passengers. The low capacity vehicles in this type can carry standee passengers if they meet provisions for low capacity standee buses.

TYPE II

Type II vehicles are those designed and constructed for inter-urban/inter-city transport without specified area for standing passengers, but can carry standing passengers over short distance in the gangway; unless otherwise prohibited by the State Transport Department.

TYPE III

Type III vehicles are those designed and constructed for long distance passenger transport, exclusively designed for comfort of seated passengers and not intended for carrying standing passengers.

TYPE IV

Type IV vehicles are those designed and constructed for special purpose use such as the following:

1. **School Bus:** means vehicles designed and constructed specially for schools, college, and other educational Institutions.
2. **Sleeper Coaches:** means vehicles designed and constructed specially berth to accommodate sleeping passengers.
3. **Tourist Bus:** means vehicles designed and constructed for the purpose of transportation of passengers as tourists and may be classified in any one Type of comfort levels.

OVERALL DIMENSIONS

Overall dimensions of the bus shall comply with the provisions laid down in Rule 93 of Central Motor Vehicle Rules, 1989, as amended from time to time.

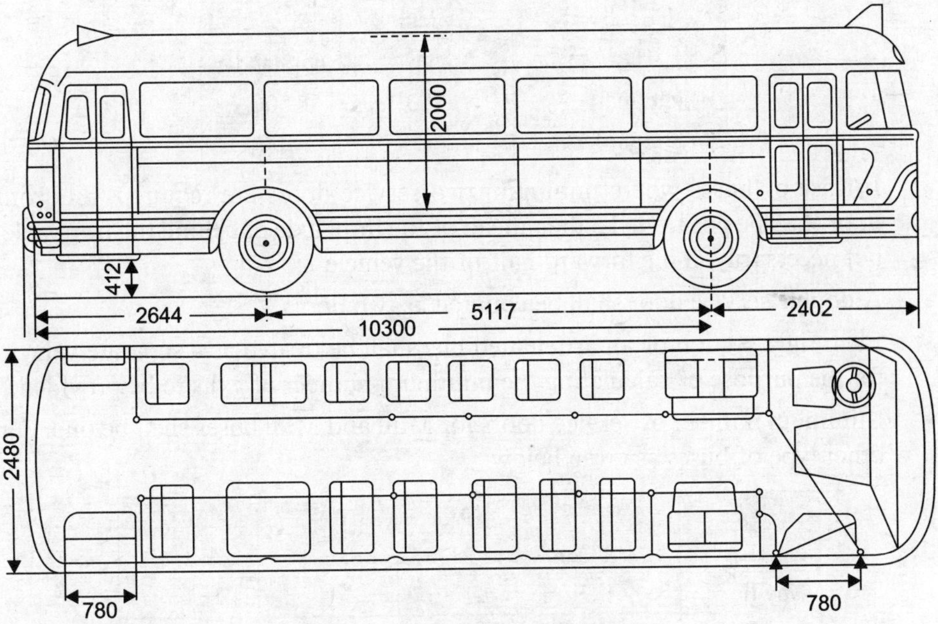

Fig.3.17: Bus dimensions (Sample)

Service doors

- The service door(s) shall be situated on the side of the vehicle that is nearer to the side of the road corresponding to the direction of traffic.
- The minimum dimensions of service doors for buses other than mini and midi buses shall be as below:

Category		Height Min. (mm)	Width Min. (mm) (As Applicable)**		
			Front	Rear	Middle#
Type I	NDX	1800	650 mm for single door and 1200 mm for double door	650 mm for single door and 1200 mm for double door	650 mm for single door and 1200 mm for double door
	SDX				
	DLX				
	ACX				
Type II	NDX	1650			—
	SDX				—
	DLX				—
	ACX				—
Type III	SDX				—
	DLX				—
	ACX				—

For mini and midi buses, the minimum dimensions of service doors as below:

	Midi & Mini Bus	
	Standee	Non Standee
Height (mm)	1650	1500
Width (mm)	650	650

- In case of buses where minimum two service doors are required, the front door shall be positioned either ahead of the front axle or behind the front axle, but necessarily in the forward half of the vehicle.
- A double service door shall be counted as two doors.
- Each rigid section of an articulated bus shall be treated as a separate vehicle for the purpose of calculating the minimum number of exits to be provided.
- Minimum number of service doors for Mini and Midi buses shall be one. For other type of buses as given below:

	NDX	SDX	DLX	ACX
Type I	2	2	1	1
Type II	1	1	1	1
Type III	N.A.	1	1	1

- In case of type I (DLX, ACX), type II and type III provision of second exit shall be optional.

Window

- Sliding type for all buses except ACX buses.
- Minimum width – 550 mm
- Minimum height

Standard bus	550 mm
Midi and mini buses	450 mm
NDX and SDX (Type I) NDX (Type II)	1000 mm
ACX	700 mm

- The above dimensions are not applicable for front and rear corner side windows, emergency exit, etc.

Emergency exit

- At least one on the opposite side of the service door.
- Minimum dimensions for Type I, Type II and Type III:

Emergency door exit	1250 mm × 550 mm
Emergency window exit	4000 cm^2

- Minimum number of emergency doors/exits or apertures (clear vision zone) except mini and midi buses:

	NDX	SDX	DLX	ACX
Type I	2	2	2	2
Type II	2	2	2	2
Type III	—	2	2	2

Steps

Dimensions of Steps in mm shall be as given in the table below:

Classes		I	II, III
First step from ground 'D'	Max. height, mm	340	380
	Min. depth, mm	300	
Other steps 'E'	Max. height, mm	250	350
	Min. height, mm	120	
	Min. depth, mm	200	

CONSTRUCTIONAL DETAILS

COMPONENTS OF BUS BODY STRUCTURE

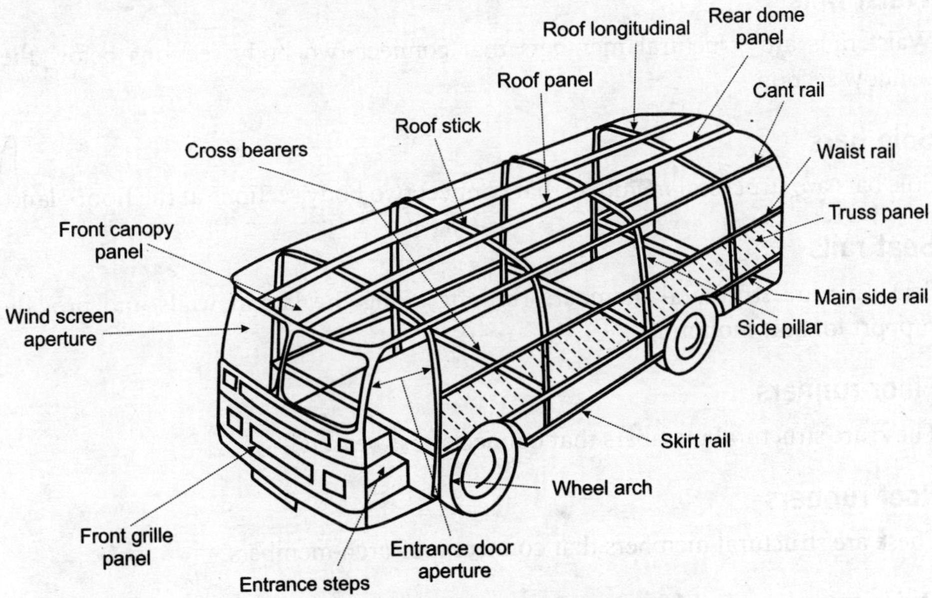

Fig.3.18: Bus body nomenclature

Cross bearers

Cross bearers are structural members mounted on the chassis frame through U-bolts or out rigger brackets. The cross bearers transmit the body load to the chassis and also withstand the forces induced during the normal operation of the vehicle.

Vertical pillars

Vertical pillars or body pillars are structural members that support the roof structure and are connected to the cross bearers through gussets. The vertical pillars transmit load to the cross bearers and also withstand the forces induced during the normal operation of the vehicle.

Roof arch members

Roof arch members are structural members that connect the vertical pillars and form a body section. In the event of a rollover, the body section absorbs the impact and provides survival protection in the passenger compartment. Gussets are also provided to improve the rigidity and strength of the body section.

Cant rails

Cant rails are structural members that connect two body sections above the window section.

Waist rails

Waist rails are structural members that connect two body sections below the window section.

Sole bars

Sole bars are structural members that connect two body sections at the floor plane.

Seat rails

Seat rails are structural members running along the lateral walls and provide support for seat mounting.

Floor runners

These are structural members that connect cross bearers.

Roof runners

These are structural members that connect roof arch members.

Out-rigger brackets

These are attachments that provide connection between the cross bearers and the chassis frame.

U-Bolts

U-Bolts are fasteners used for fastening the cross bearers to the chassis frame.

A-Pillar

A-Pillar means any roof support forward of seating reference point.

Front outrigger members

Front Outrigger Members are provided to transfer load of Body structure members. These are fixed to the chassis side members. "A" pillars are supported on outrigger members such that the roof load is transferred to the chassis load bearing members. Further in the event of a collision the energy is absorbed by the pillars and the out riggers and minimise the impact energy transmitted to the driver and passenger compartment (Protection against frontal collision).

DESIGN OF INTEGRAL BUS

Chassis under structure

The following loads are considered for designing the under structure.

a. Unit weights like engine, gearbox, radiator, steering box, batteries and fuel tank acting as paint loads at the mounting points.

b. Weight of understructure considered as uniformly distributed load.

Considering vertical and integral bending, the maximum bending moment is calculated and a section required to carry the weights is decided allowing for a reserve factor, depending on the road conditions.

Chassis body structure

The loads considered for body structure are:

a. Body weight considered as uniformly distributed load.

b. Payload considered as uniformly distributed load.

Considering bending, torsion and combined bending and torsion loads, the body structure is designed allowing for a reserve factor depending on the road conditions. Presently, the stress analysis of the design under structure and body structure is being carried out using finite element techniques and SAP-IV program.

To sun up the general merits and faults of the various designs of coaches, it can be said that the coaches easiest to design are of integral construction with the engine either at the rear or placed under the floor.

SEQUENCE OF BUS BUILDING OPERATION

1. Chassis Preparation
2. Side and front framing

3. Roof framing and rear end
4. Truss panel riveted
5. General inspection
6. Roof panels
7. Paneling and moulding
8. Final finish

Chassis Preparation

The floor frame is placed in position, holding down bolds fixed and all parts of the chassis painted.

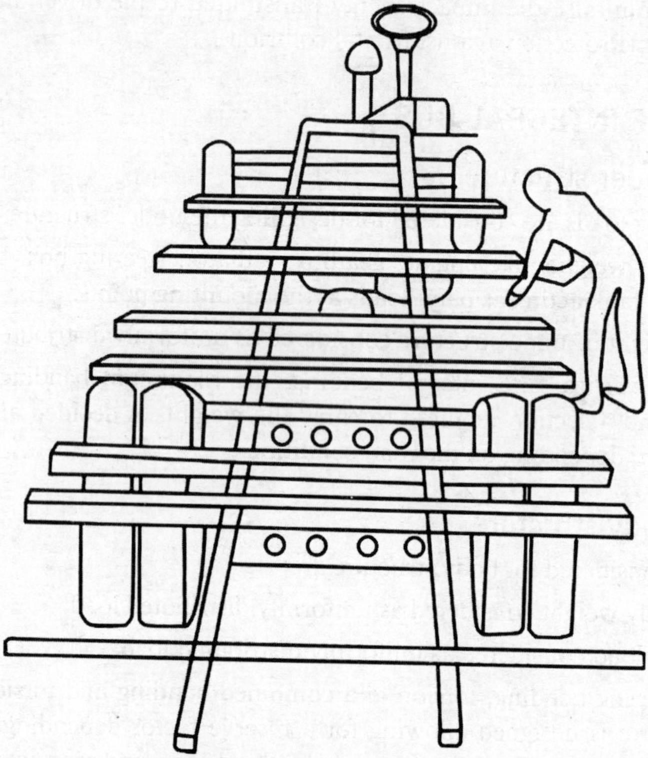

Fig.3.19: Chassis preparation

Side and front framing

The body side framing and front end is assembled. Truss panels bolted into position, the body lined up with the waist rail and the lower bolts tightened.

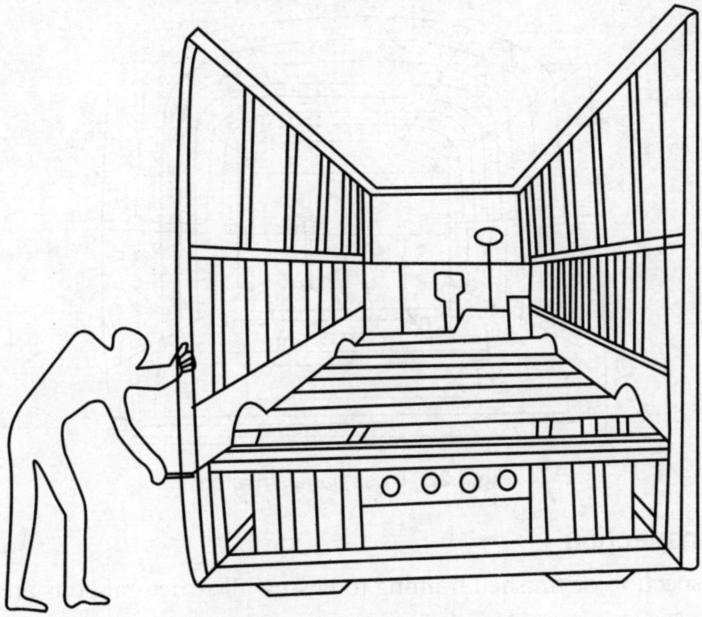

Fig.3.20: Side and front framing

Roof framing and rear end

The body ends and roof framing are positioned and fixed, the wheel boxes and entrance steps installed.

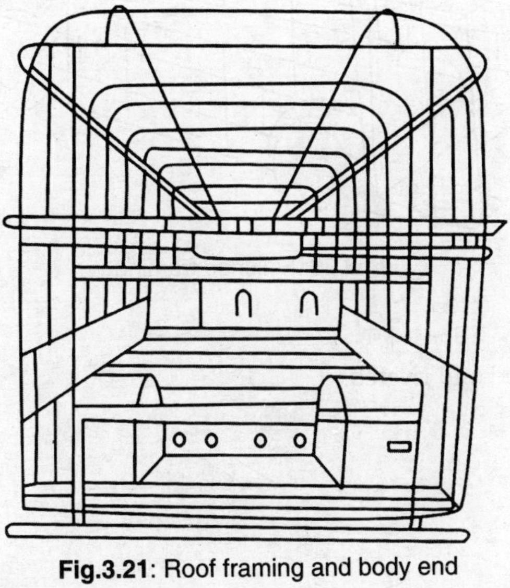

Fig.3.21: Roof framing and body end

Truss panel riveted

Truss panels between the waist rail and seat rail over the wheel arches are riveted into position.

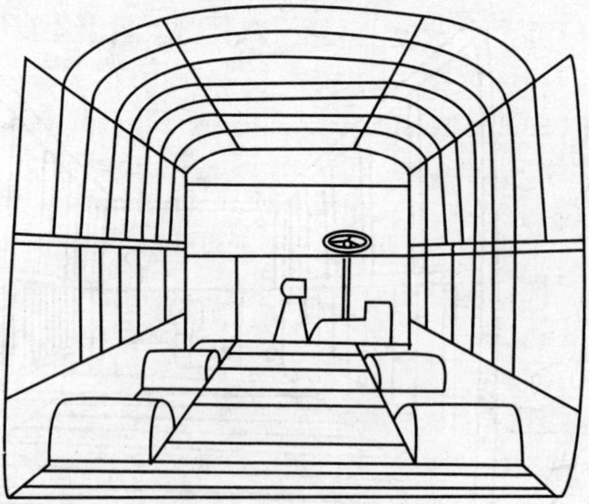

Fig.3.22: Truss panels riveted

General inspection

General inspection of finished framing to ensure all structural bolts are tight and truss panels securely riveted.

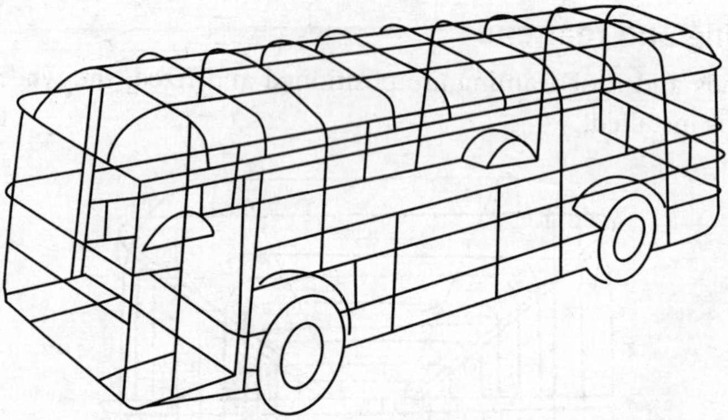

Fig.3.23: Finished framing

Roof panels

Roof panels are fixed and riveted.

Fig.3.24: Roof panel

Panelling and moulding

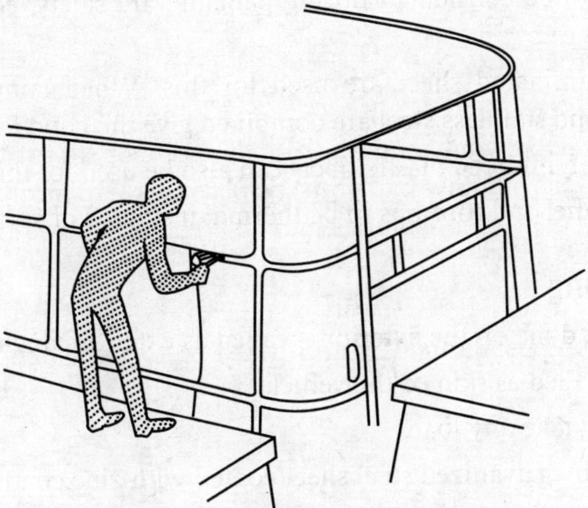

Fig.3.25: Panelling and moulding

Final finish

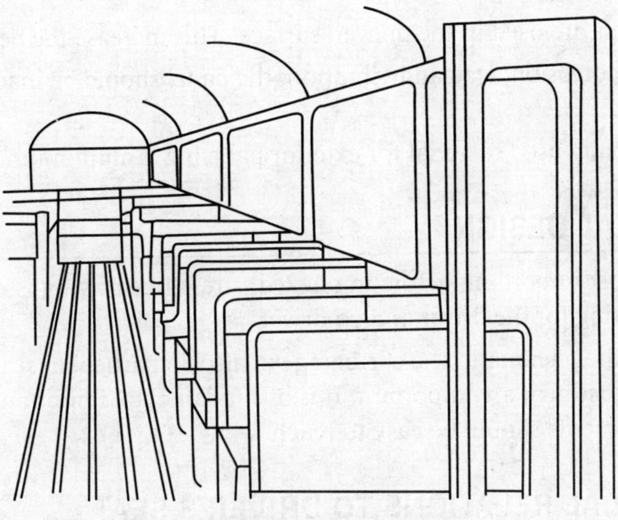

Fig.3.26: Final finishing

DOUBLE SKIN CONSTRUCTION

Normally inner skin will take part in load carrying, outer skin will be fixed in such a way that it can be replaced easily.

Interior paneling

- This is the paneling done inside the vehicle.

- The paneling inside the body gives comfort to the passengers.
- The factors to be considered during paneling are safety, easy maintenance, easy cleaning.
- Decorated laminated sheet are used for this. When laminated sheet and aluminium and stainless steel are combined give the good look.
- GRPF (glass reinforced plastic fiber) can also be used for this purpose.
- Floor side panel and roof has to be thermal insulated or sprayed.

Exterior paneling

- The paneling done on the exterior is called as exterior paneling.
- This is also called as skin of the vehicle.
- This does not take any load.
- This is done by galvanized steel sheet coated with zinc coating.
- The galvanized steel sheet is welded or riveted to form panel.
- The body paneling is done by two ways.
- Small panels are attached together according to the requirement.
- To make a single big panel for the whole length.
- Steel sheets are used in the uneven surface. This increase the beauty.
- To avoid corrosion, leak and vibration, the panel should be made with plastic trim fillet.
- The normally used material for exterior paneling is aluminium.

DRIVER SEAT DESIGN

One of the most important factors in relaxed, stress free driving is ergonomically optimized seating for the driver and co-driver.

Not only the pneumatic seat springing but also, in particular, seat position and convenient adjustment are important. It is of fundamental importance too that all the control elements should be easy to reach.

GEOMETRICAL RELATIONS TO DRIVER'S SEAT

A correct driving position is important in the vehicle layout and the seat position in relation to the steering wheel, foot controls and other secondary controls is of fundamental importance in body design. Seating position has an influence not only on the driver's comfort but also on road safety. The following points are to be considered in designing the driver's seat.

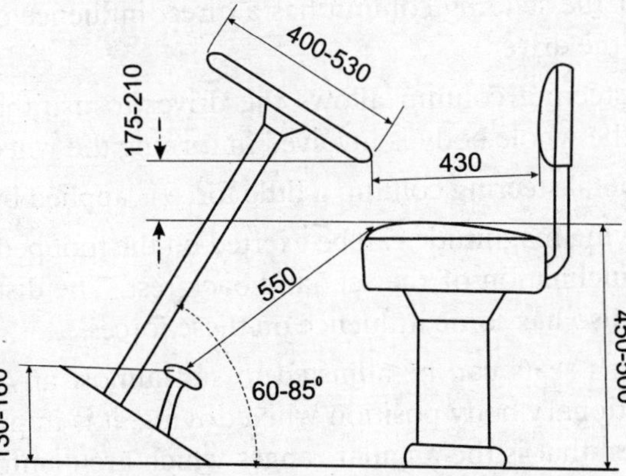

Fig.3.27: Bus seating position

- The driver's seat should be adjustable 45 mm horizontally and 30 mm vertically.
- The most comfortable position of the body is achieved when the bulk of weight is taken by ischial bones. A more slanted body position will cause abnormal tension in the pelvis muscles leading to tiredness.
- The back-rest must support the trunk in a vertical position and that the upper part of the back-rest props up the upper position of the spine and ensures the correct position of the trunk, with a pushed out and extended thorax and the shoulders slightly lowered. An uncomfortable back-rest results in compression of the thorax, which makes breathing difficult.
- A good back-rest relieves the neck and shoulder muscles and must therefore, depend on the size of the individual. Thus it is advisable to use an adjustable back rest.
- The angle between the seat and back-rest must be obtuse, although less for the driver than for the passenger seats.
- Arm rests reduce tiredness if their position does not cause the track to bend or stretch.
- It is important to avoid acute angles between the truck and pelvis, since the knees become raised and the thighs press on the stomach. This can be caused by any of the following:
    a. The seat being tilted too much
    b. Insufficient room for the legs
    c. An unsuitable angle between the seat and the back-rest
- The seat cushions should be fairly rigid and must have sufficient shock absorbing qualities to prevent resonance of spring.
- Numbness in the calves of the legs and in the feet is caused by the front edge of the seat exerting too great pressure on the lower part of the thigh. This results from excessive height of the seat or a hollow seat.

Inclination of the steering column has a direct influence on the force which can be applied by the driver.

a. Vertical steering column allows the driver to use the maximum force because the whole body is involved in turning the wheel.

b. In horizontal steering column a little force is applied by the shoulders.

Forces of varying magnitude can be exerted on the foot pedals, depending on the angles of the inclination of the seat and back-rest. The distance between the floor and the seat also has some influence on these forces.

Modern driver's seats can be adjusted to suit almost any driver. Given the predominantly stationary body position when driving, it is important to maintain the 'comfort angles' that is the angular ranges which are comfortable for human joints. The seats that are now usually fitted, some of which are pneumatically sprung, provide all the adjustment necessary. Good lateral support against lateral acceleration makes driving easier while restraint systems improve safety.

Passenger seat

All the considerations for the design of driver's seat apply to passenger seat except inclination of back-rest. The inclination of the back-rest of passenger seats can be arranged to give a more reclining position than that used for the driver seat. Journey time determines the degree of comfort. The increase in comfort usually provided as the journey time is increased.

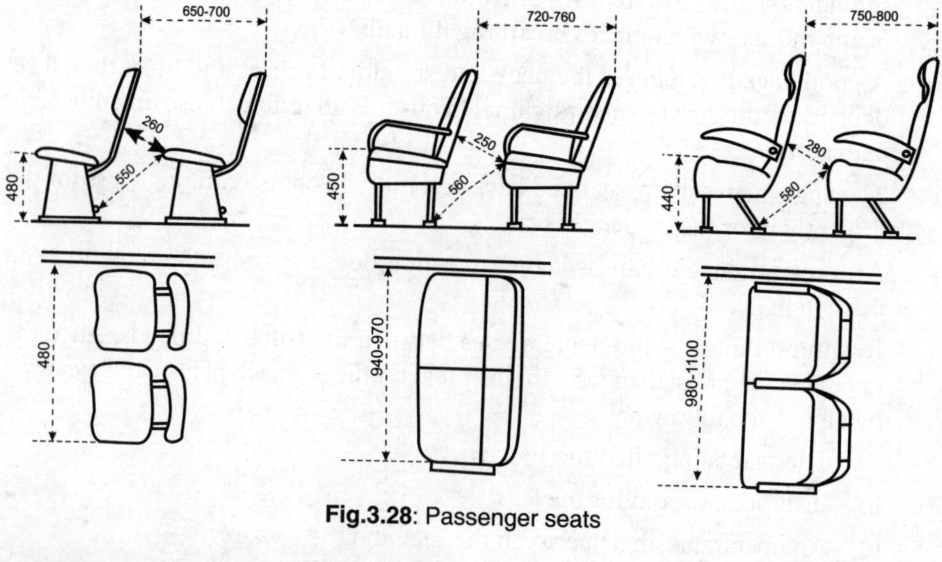

Fig.3.28: Passenger seats

SAFETY ASPECT OF BUS BODY

Vehicle evacuation

Vehicle bodies shall be designed and constructed so as to enable the vehicle to be operated in a safe and stable manner, even at full capacity. Suitable provisions shall be made to ensure safe access to and exit from the vehicle, particularly in case of emergency.

Road adherence

The vehicles should be equipped with Electronic Stability Program and Tyre pressure monitoring system in order to guarantee an optimum pressure to maximize the safety and provide eco-performance.

Driver's vision

Mirrors between the door and the wheel as well as the horizontal mirrors in front should be mandatory for all buses to improve the indirect visibility of people getting on and off. Windows condensation requirement for buses and coaches should be similar to that of private cars. Mirror design can be improved to eliminate blind spots.

Reverse assist system

The buses can be equipped with reverse assist system for rearward visibility and safety consideration.

Prevent fire propagation

The materials used for bus body should be capable of preventing or at least retard fire in order to allow the occupants to evacuate the vehicle in the event of fire. The engine compartment can also be equipped with fire detection system also emergency exits must be provided in the bus body.

Ergonomically designed dash board

Dashboards differ with different vehicles based on the type. Dashboards should be provided with ease to identify all the controls, dials and warning devices.

Seat design

Seat design can be improved to increase safety. Suspension seats can improve comfort and therefore, reduce tiredness for long distance transport. However, the safety benefits do not extend to urban driving, where infrastructure traffic calming measures (i.e speed bumps) may create safety hazard. The position of the upper belt: effective anchorage must be permanently marked in the vehicle or seat defining the child position or adult position, which allocates the upper anchorage safety belt at the level of occupants shoulder automatically.

Emergency lights

Emergency lights must be provided for all bus bodies in case of any emergency situation.

Intelligent transport system

Bus bodies can be equipped with intelligent transport system like GPS in order to track the vehicle and for safety considerations.

Review Questions

Short Questions

1. What do you mean by double skin construction?
2. How the floor height does influences the bus body layout.
3. Mention the advantages and disadvantages of integral bus body.
4. Classify the bus based on shape and style.
5. Classify the bus bodies based on capacity.
6. List the safety aspects of bus body.
7. What are the advantages of two level single deck buses?
8. What are the possible locations of engine in a bus body layout?
9. Define and identify the following: Back light, Cant panel, Scuttle panel and Rain cutter:Sill panel
10. Define and identify:
11. Indicate the special features of Limousine, Articulate bus and Traveling shop with neat sketches.
12. With a sketch indicate bus body regulation.
13. What are the different types of metal sections that are being used in bus body construction?
14. Differentiate double decker and articulate bus with neat sketches.

Long Questions

1. Describe the various types of bus body with sketches.
2. Explain the construction of a single deck bus with sketches.
3. How does the entrance and exit location influence the bus body layout?
4. Explain the constructional details of a conventional bus body.
5. Explain the design and construction of an Integral bus.
6. Compare integral and conventional bus body construction with examples.
7. Explain the different types of metal sections used in body construction along with their merits and demerits.
8. Write a note on floor height and engine location in the case of bus body construction.

4 Commercial Vehicle Details

COMMERCIAL VEHICLE BODIES

Commercial vehicle bodies are constructed either as open trucks or closed vans.

BASED ON ENGINE MOUNTING

Commercial vehicles are classified into two basic groups according to engine mounting: normal control and forward control.

Normal control type

The normal control vehicle has the engine located in front of the driver's cab and is not as widely used today.

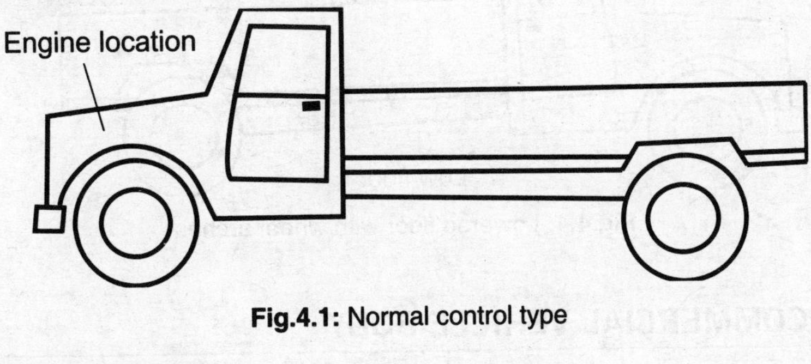

Fig.4.1: Normal control type

Forward control type

In the forward control type, the engine is positioned either in or below the driver's cab.

Fig.4.2: Forward control type

BASED ON LOAD-CARRYING PLATFORM

With regard to the load-carrying platform there are two types: normal flat floor and lowered floor with wheel arches. In addition, body sides of any height, either fixed or movable, may be provided.

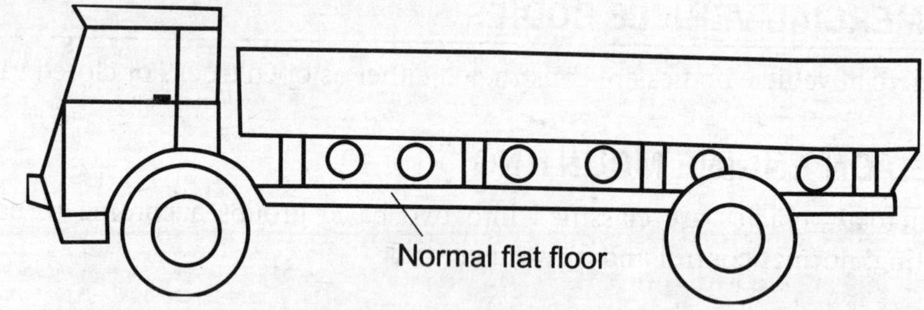

Fig.4.3: Normal flat floor

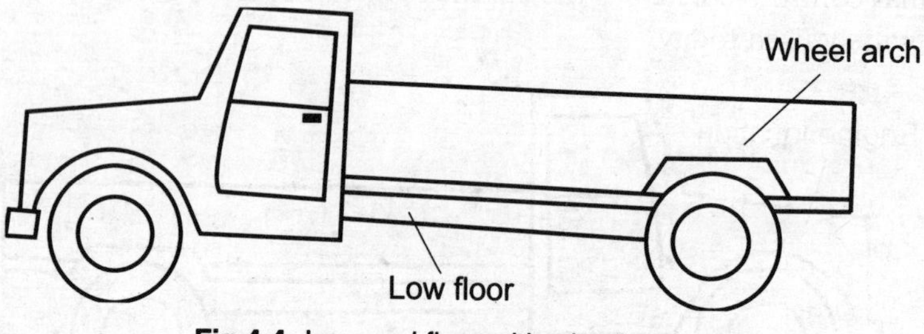

Fig.4.4: Lowered floor with wheel arches

LIGHT COMMERCIAL VEHICLE BODY

Commercial vehicle bodies are constructed either as open trucks or closed vans. Vans or small commercial vehicles are most frequently used for the transport of readymade commercial goods. The design of the body of a van should take into consideration the need to ensure suitable conditions for the transport of the goods (leak-proof interior, ventilation, and temperature) and also consider the conditions of loading and unloading.

The need for specialization in transport has created the demand for a whole group of commercial vehicle bodies which can be classified according to their functions.

BASED ON THEIR FUNCTIONS

Universal

The most popular is the two or three-door general purpose van known as the 'universal'.

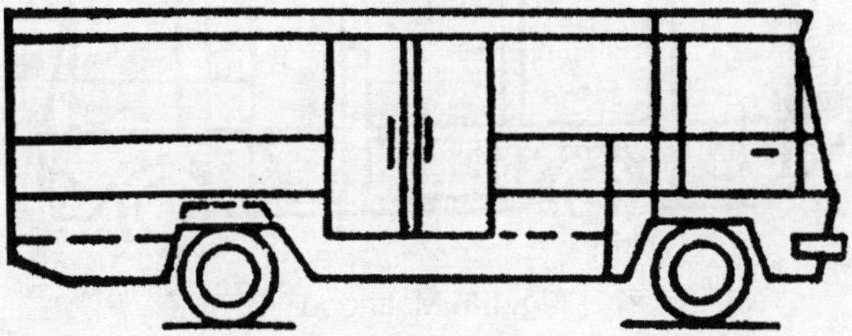

Fig.4.5: Universal

Under-floor box

To increase the load-carrying surface, vans are often equipped with either under-floor boxes.

Fig.4.6: Under-floor box

Sliding type

For ease of loading the side door can be of the sliding type.

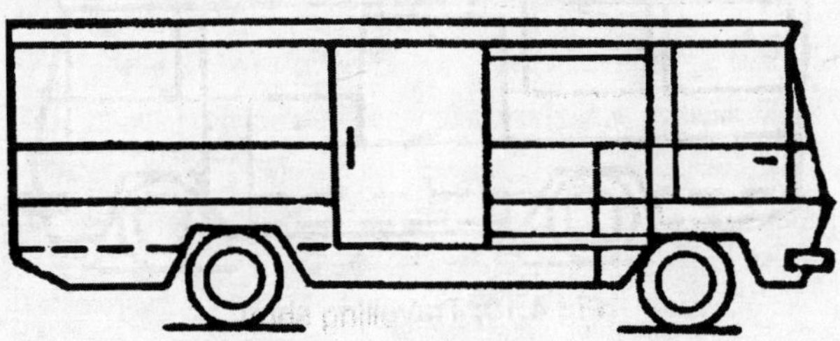

Fig.4.7: Sliding type

BASED ON THEIR PURPOSES

The three types of vans mentioned can be used for different purposes, depending on the fittings inside.

Multi-door

For very specialist loads such as bakery, or other edible goods, etc, multi-door vans with under-floor shelves and drawers are used.

Fig.4.8: Multi-door

Raised roof

For transportation of large articles vans with a raised roof are used.

Fig.4.9: Raised roof

Service van

Service vans are equipped according to their function, such as travelling shops with adequate display windows and counters, or travelling workshops having additional lighting by means of roof lights.

Fig.4.10: Travelling shop

Fig.4.11: Travelling workshop

BASED ON DRIVER CAB DESIGN

Forward control integral van

The forward control integral van is the type where the driver's cab is in one-piece with the load-carrying compartment (integral type) or where the load-carrying compartment is separated from the driver's cab.

The integral type is an economical type as it is suitable for mass production.

Fig.4.12: Integral type

Fig.4.13: Separate driver's cab and load-carrying compartment

Open commercial type

Open commercial vehicle bodies can be made with lowered floors or raised floors. Raised floor vehicles are normally provided with under-floor compartments.

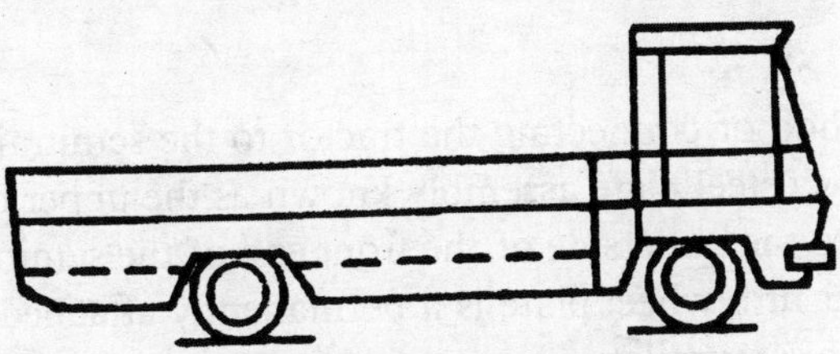

Fig.4.14: Lowered floor type

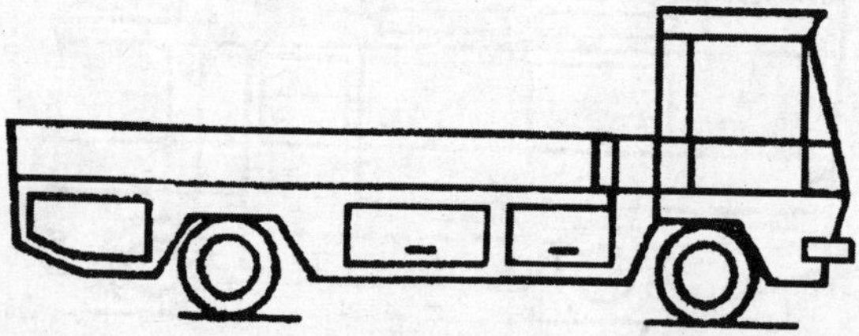

Fig.4.15: Raised floor with under-floor compartments

Refrigeration type

Some vehicles are built with refrigeration and the vans are used for this work may be classified as follows:

1. No thermal insulation
2. With thermal insulation, the so-called 'half isothermal' van.
3. With thermal insulation and specially designed bodywork to avoid 'thermal bridges'. These bodies are called 'isothermal'.

The isothermal body construction is used for completely refrigerated vehicles with their own refrigeration unit which maintains the temperature below 0°C.

FLAT PLATFORM BODY

A flat bed truck is made up of a chassis fitted with a platform body on which goods are carried. Cargo is secured on the deck with ropes or sheeting. Flat beds are flexible and can accommodate many different types of loads.

TRAILER

A trailer or semi-trailer is a cargo vehicle with no motive power of its own, towed by a motor vehicle. These vehicles are provided with a drawbar or tongue for attachment to a coupling mounted on the towing vehicle. Motor vehicles specially designed for towing trailers or semitrailers are known as *tractors*.

Considerable time must be spent in loading and unloading certain types of cargos. Trailers are useful in such cases because they can be left at the loading and unloading points while the tractor tows other loads.

CONSTRUCTION

Fifth wheel

The standard method of connecting the tractor to the semitrailer is by means of a *fifth wheel*. A heavy steel plate assembly known as the upper fifth wheel plate, is securely attached to the underside of the front end of the semitrailer frame. In the center of the upper fifth wheel plate is a permanently attached kingpin by which the tractor pulls the semitrailer.

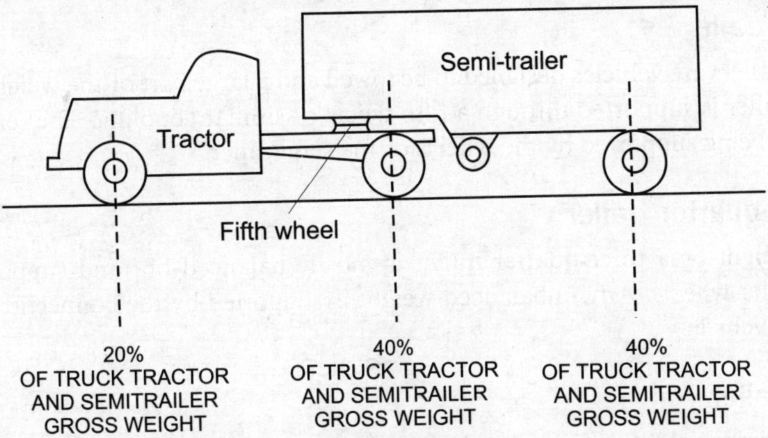

Fig.4.16: Fifth wheel

Suspension

Trailer spring suspension is the same as that employed on motor vehicles. Auxiliary springs are often used. Radius rods are usually used to maintain axle alignment and to transmit braking and pulling action between the trailer axle and frame. The wheels are usually slightly cambered.

Braking system

Air, vacuum or electric braking systems are used with trailers. The trailer braking system is coupled to that of the towing vehicle by a flexible hose and detachable couplings or cables. The trailer braking system is usually designed so that the brakes are applied and keep the trailer in place when these couplings are disconnected. However, when the trailer is detached from the towing vehicle, the trailer brakes will hold for only a limited time. For this reason, wheel blocks are usually used to keep the trailer in place when it is to be idle for some time. Provisions are often made for carrying wheel blocks on a trailer.

TYPES OF TRAILERS

Trailers are of three general types, depending on the manner in which their weight is supported: semitrailer, three-quarter trailer and full trailer.

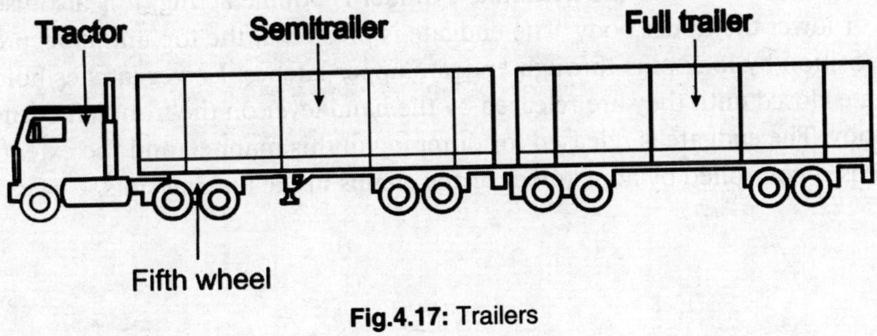

Fig.4.17: Trailers

Semi-trailer

Semitrailers are vehicles designed to be towed and a large part of the weight of the semitrailer is supported through a fifth wheel or similar coupling. The remainder weight being supported by the wheels of the semitrailer.

Three-quarter trailer

The weight of a three-quarter trailer is mostly balanced on, and supported by the trailer wheels. Any unbalanced weight is supported by the connection to the towing vehicle.

Full trailer

The entire weight of a full trailer is supported by the trailer wheels.

TIPPER

Tippers have an open top steel body that can be raised (using a hydraulic arm) at its front end, thus enabling a load to be discharged. Typical loads include aggregates such as soil, sand and stone. These trucks are also referred to as *Dumpers*.

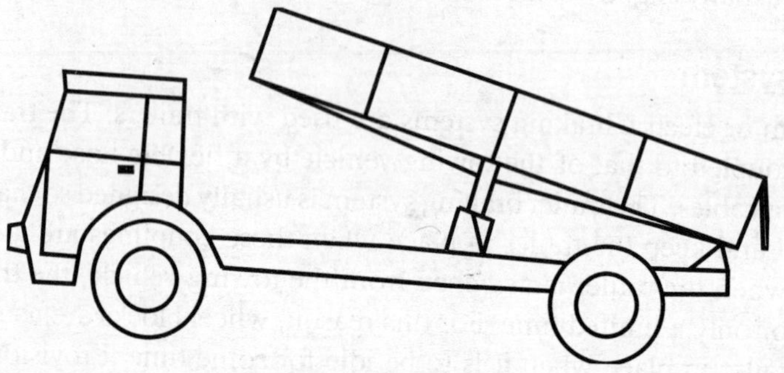

Fig.4.18: Tipper

CONSTRUCTION

The tipper body pivots at the rear. The pressure developed in the hydraulic hoist cylinder by the operation of a special pump causes the dump body to move up as shown in Fig.4.18 Since the hydraulic cylinder is double acting, it is also used to hold or lower the tipper body. The endgate is pivoted at the top and is secured in this position by lock pins through endgate upper latches. Lower latches hold the endgate closed until they are released by the hand lever on the front left corner of the body. The endgate is released for dumping in this manner, and the extent that it opens is controlled by adjustment of the chains in the locking slots.

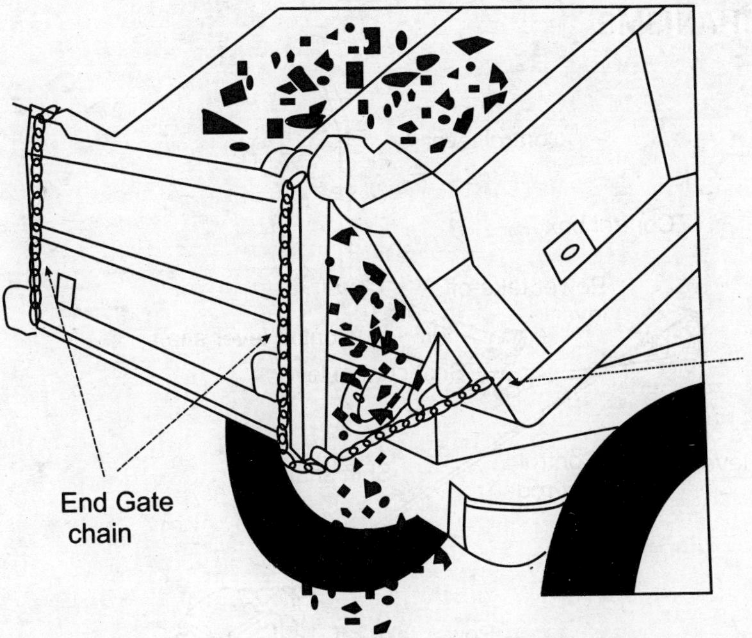

Fig.4.19: End gate

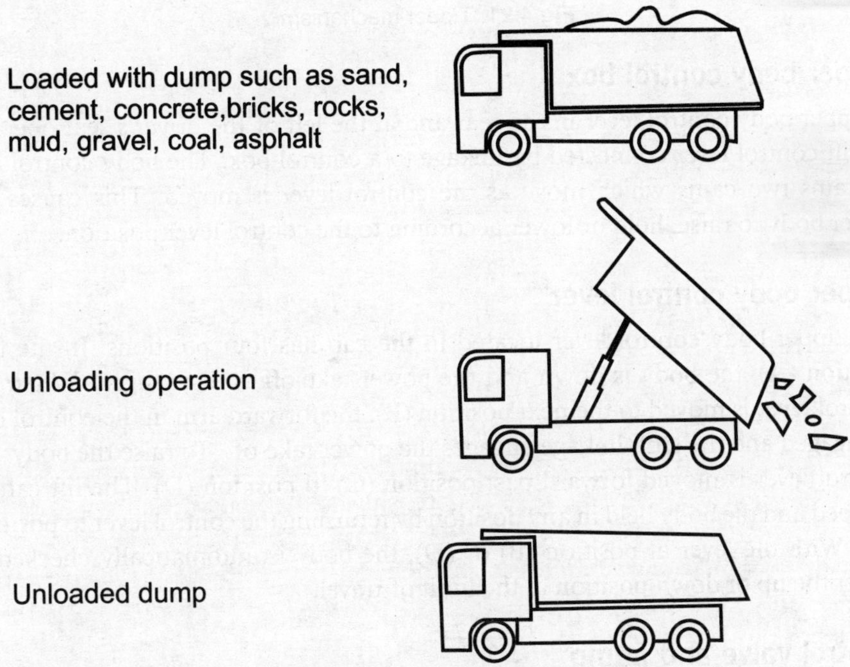

Fig.4.20: Operation of a tipper

TIPPER MECHANISMS

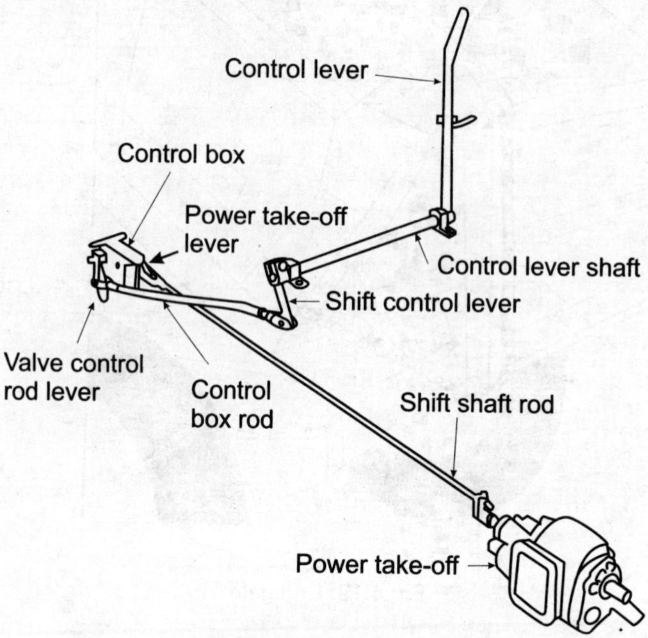

Fig.4.21: Tipper mechanism

Tipper body control box

A tipper body control lever in the rear and at the left of the driver's seat operates a shift control lever connected by linkage to a control box. The body control box contains two cams which move as the control lever is moved. This causes the tipper body to raise, hold or lower according to the control lever position.

Tipper body control lever

The tipper body control lever located in the cab has four positions. In the first position (A), the body is down and the power take-off is disengaged. When the control lever is moved to the next position (B), the forward arm in the control box is engaged and the shift linkage engages the power take-off. To raise the body, the control lever is moved forward past position (C) to position (D). The lift can be stopped and the body held in any position by returning the control lever to position (C). With the lever at position (B) or (D), the body is automatically checked at either the up or down position at the limit of travel.

Control valve and pump

When the power take-off is engaged, the pump is driven. It can now deliver hydraulic fluid to the hydraulic cylinder. The control valve is linked to the control lever. When the control lever is moved to position D, the control valve directs the hydraulic fluid from the pump into the front or elevating end of the hydraulic cylinder. The hydraulic pressure forces the piston and piston rod toward the rear of the truck. This raises the tipper body.

Hydraulic cylinder

The hydraulic cylinder is double acting and is mounted in the forward part of the truck subframe. The cylinder base is mounted on a shaft held in bearings on the inner side of the subframe. The piston rod is connected to a crosshead which is pivoted with a roller arm on each end. Arms are supported by bearing pins on the bottom of the body. The free ends of the arms are equipped with rollers which engage curved ramps attached to the sides of the subframe. The movement of the piston rod, carried through the arms and rollers to the ramps, raises the body.

CLASSIFICATION

Based on type of tipping method

- Hydraulic
- Electric

Based on location of tipping mechanism

- Front end tipping
- Under body tipping

Based on direction of unloading

- Single way
- Three way

TANKER BODY

Road tankers have a permanent tank fitted to the chassis for the transportation of liquids, gases or powders. Tankers are of two general types: tank semitrailers and tank trucks.

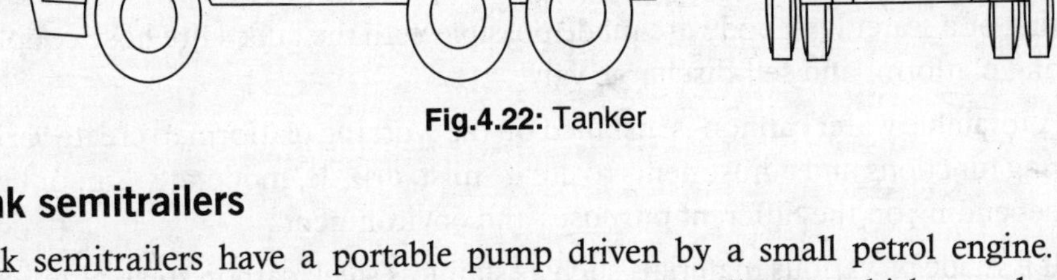

Fig.4.22: Tanker

Tank semitrailers

Tank semitrailers have a portable pump driven by a small petrol engine. The pump can be used to unload or load the tank, depending on which way the hose connections are made to the pump and tank. The pump is usually driven by a single-cylinder, 4-stroke petrol engine.

Tank trucks

On the tank truck the power take-off, which is mounted on the transfer assembly, contains a pump drive. When the driver positions the controls, the pumping equipment is set into operation. At the same time, an auxiliary engine governor comes into action to properly limit engine speed during the time that the pumping equipment is operated. This prevents over speeding of the engine.

CLASSIFICATION OF TANKER BODY

According to the type of liquid carrying

a. Water tank body

b. Fuel tank body

c. Chemical liquids tank body

According to the shape of the tanker body

a. Circular (round) cross section

b. Elliptical cross section

According to bulkheads

a. Baffled tanks

b. Un baffled tanks (smooth bore tanks)

ACCORDING TO THE TYPE OF LIQUID CARRYING

Water tank body

It is mainly composed of the truck chassis, water inlet, outlet system and the water tank body.

It is a cylindrical, horizontal tank mounted onto the truck chassis A water tank truck is mostly used for storing water and transporting the same to some places where there is an urgent need for water.

A sprinkler water tank truck is used for making the city environment clean and beautiful by cleaning and watering the streets, plants, and grass.

Water tank trucks have different volume capacity. The rear sprinkler, and side spraying of a water tank body are made possible with the tank's fire hose coupling, working platform, and self-discharge valve.

A rotatable water cannon is installed on the working platform to create various spraying functions and adjustments to create mist, drizzle, moderate rain, or heavy rain depending on the different purposes and environment.

It is made of various materials such as stainless steel, carbon steel, aluminum, and fiberglass-reinforced plastic.

The rigid steel body is further sprayed with superior quality special paint to allow it to be more solid and safe.

Fuel tank truck

It is constructed in such a way to safely carry different kinds of fuel to and from its destination.

Some fuel tank body are used to transport different grades of fuel to and from the gasoline station can be

- insulated or non-insulated,
- pressurized or non-pressurized,
- single or multiple compartments.

Some of the materials used to build these fuel tanks include aluminum, fiberglass reinforced plastic or FRP, stainless steel, and carbon steel.

Insulated tank is used to minimize fuel temperature increases inside the tank, reducing fuel loss due to evaporation.

The fuel tank body that carries these flammable gases is often pressurized and can carry around 1,000 to 3,000 gallons of this fuel at one time.

Some fuel tanks can be compartmentalised to carry 2, 3, 4, or 5 different kinds of fuel at one time in one cylindrical containment unit.

Chemical liquids tank body

Chemical liquid tank truck is designed to carry corrosive, hazardous chemical liquids.

It is mainly composed of a chassis, tank body, discharge system, as well as some protective devices.

The tank can be constructed of carbon steel, stainless steel, aluminum alloy, or other materials, according to the specific properties of the transporting medium.

Some tank trucks can carry a variety of products at once due to their internal divisions in their tank, allowing for an increased number of delivery options.

ACCORDING TO THE SHAPE OF THE TANKER BODY

Circular cross section

Circular cross section is readily adaptable to frameless construction.

When a circular tank is inclined towards the rear the center of gravity can be equal to that of an elliptical tank.

Elliptical section

- Elliptical tank is used for a wide range of purposes, Elliptical tanks are a popular form for tanks that hold large volumes of liquids.

- Low center of gravity
- Capacity
  - A tank made in an elliptical shape provides a low center of gravity when it is placed on its side.
  - For holding large loads of liquids, that distribution of a tank's contents is particularly effective at providing stability.
  - The low center of gravity also allows tanks located on truck trailers to sit lower to the ground, providing better sight lines for truck drivers.
  - An elliptical tank has significantly greater capacity than a round tank with the same diameter.

ACCORDING TO BULKHEADS

Some large tanks are divided into several smaller tanks by bulkheads. Bulkheads are liquid-tight separators between compartments inside the tank.

Baffled tanks

Some tanks have compartments in them that have holes. If the compartment walls have holes in them, they are called baffles.

Baffles let the liquid flow through and help control the forward and backward liquid surge when the vehicle is travelling, especially at higher speeds.

However, side to side surge can still occur which can cause a rollover.

It is used in fuel transporters to ensure safe handling.

Un-baffled tanks

Un-baffled tanks are also known as Smooth bore tanks. They have nothing inside to slow down the flow of the liquid. Therefore, forward and back surge is very strong.

Smooth bore tanks are usually transport food products, sanitation, and corrosive liquids.

DESIGN CONSIDERATIONS

The security of the discharge hoses provide ample drain holes to enable the liquid to drain away rather than to remain inside the container.

Selection of material for the right tank

a. When corrosive liquids are to be carried, the material must resist their corrosive action and stainless steel be used.

b. To provide a none reactive surface to the load and for cleanness', metals such as zinc, aluminium, cadmium, and copper.

Aluminium has long been used for fabricating tankers to carry liquids such as petrol and fuel oils largely on account of its weight/strength relationship which makes possible an uplift of between 5% and 8% carrying capacity when compared with a similar construction in steel.

DIMENSIONS OF DRIVER'S SEAT IN RELATION TO CONTROLS

- Inclination of the steering column has a direct influence on the force which can be applied by the driver. A vertical steering column allows the driver to use the maximum force because the whole body is involved in the work of turning the wheel.
- Trucks have controls which require large forces and it is therefore usual to find vertical steering columns and a seating position that allows the driver to exert his full weight on the pedals.
- Since pressure on the driver's thigh from the front edge of the seat causes tiredness, the inclination of the seat decreases as the height of the seat from the floor increases.
- The inclination of the back-rest also depends on this height and the inter-related figures given in Table 4.1. The angle of the back-rest is further limited by the angle between the line of sight and the road surface.

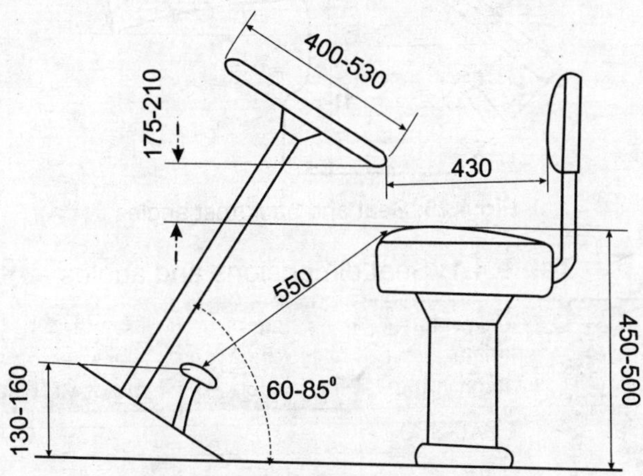

Fig.4.23: Heavy forward control

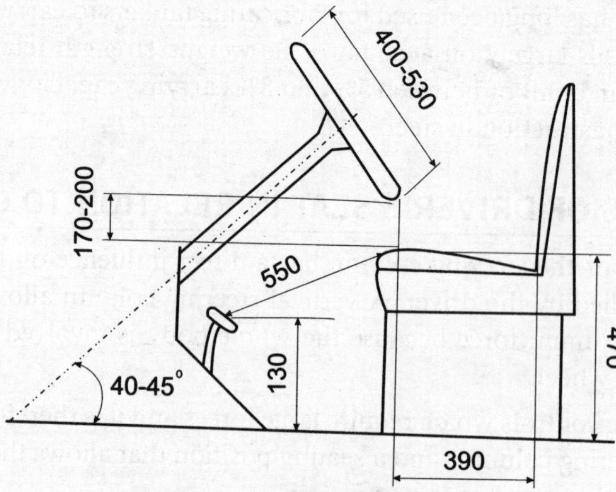

Fig.4.24: Heavy normal control

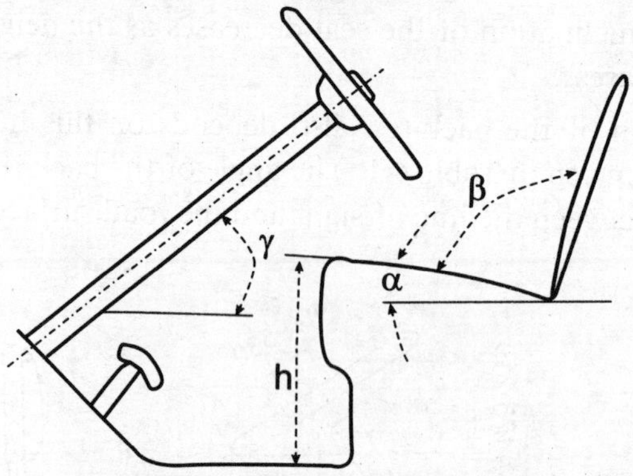

Fig.4.25: Seat and back-rest angles

Table 4.1: Seat dimensions and angles

Class of vehicle	Cushion height above floor, h mm	Angle of cushion inclination, °α	Angle of back-rest inclination, °β	Maximum force on pedal, P kg
Light commercial	340-380	10	98	70
Normal control truck	400-470	9	96	74
Forward control truck	430-500	7	92	82

DRIVERS CAB

The relative positions of the main components must be fixed as the first stage of design of a commercial vehicle.

HEAVY COMMERCIAL VEHICLES

The driver and crew can be placed in one of four basic positions in relation to the engine.

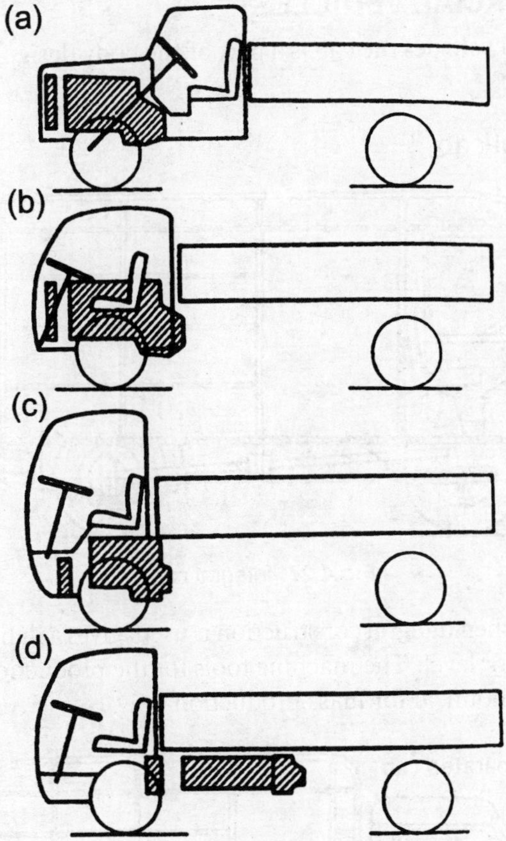

Fig.4.26: Truck cabs

(a) Normal control

In the classic or normal control type, the driver and crew are placed behind the engine.

(b) Forward control with engine above front axle

In this forward control type, driver and crew sit beside the engine.

(c) Forward control with lowered engine

Another alternative in a forward control vehicle is that the driver and crew sit above the engine. This allows a cab to accommodate 3 or 4 persons.

(d) Forward control with under floor engine

If the engine located under the floor, the result is a spacious cab with the sources of noise and heat eliminated. In addition, such a cab structure is much simpler as the more complicated floor and engine bonnet are avoided.

LIGHT COMMERCIAL VEHICLES

In light commercial vehicles the cab is a part of the body design (van) or a separate body (pickup).

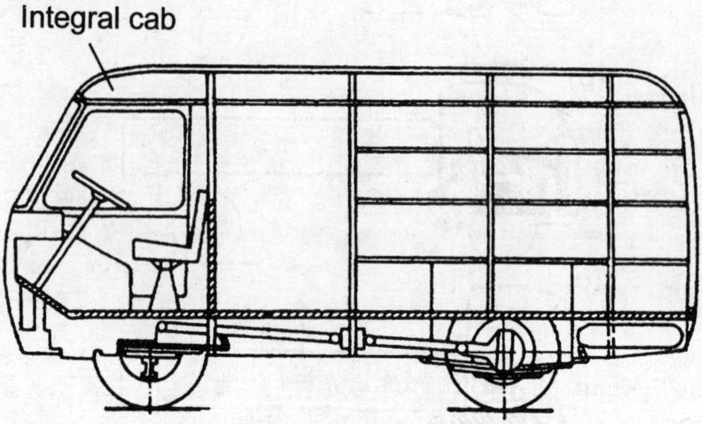

Fig.4.27: Integral cab

The first type, when integral construction is used, gives a lighter, more compact van with a lower floor level. The machine tools for the production of this type cab are suitable and economical for mass production only.

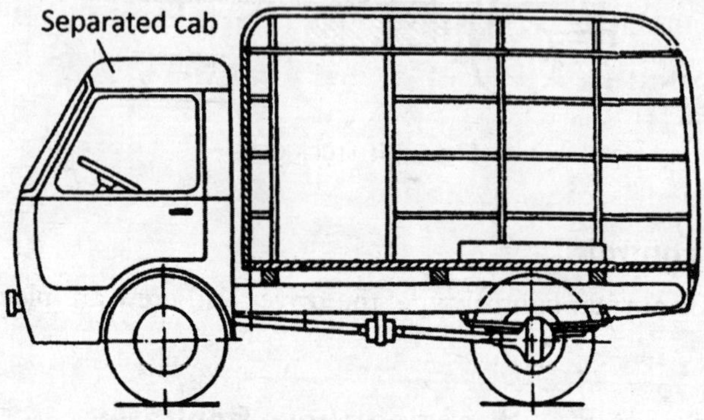

Fig.4.28: Separated cab

The type with a separate cab is heavier, less compact and generally has a higher floor level. In spite of these disadvantages, it is economic in cases of individual or small series production using readymade, mass produced body components. These components, which may be the longitudinal members, junction sections, etc., are usually made of light alloy.

DRIVERS CAB DESIGN

The shape of the cab must comply with the geometric parameters such as the height of steps, position of driver, downward and upward visibility, inclination of the windscreen, ventilation openings, size of doors, movement functions of driver, safety of work, etc.

Compactness of the driver's cab is one of the main aims of design. A compact cab is not only lighter and cheaper but also makes the whole vehicle more economic by increasing the area to be utilised for carrying load.

Sleeper cab

Only in the case of the cab of a lorry which is designed for long distance journeys, cab length can be extended to l_2. This loss of space is compensated for by non-stop running trucks i.e. one driver drives the vehicle while the other rests on a folding bed.

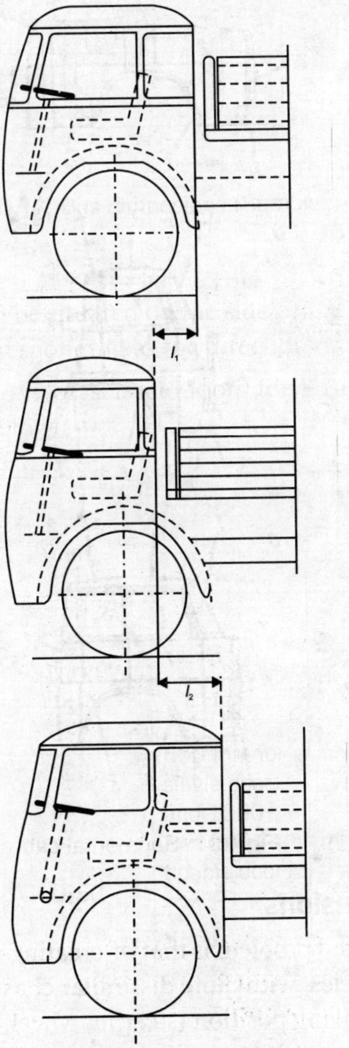

Fig.4.29: Sleeper cabs

Segment design

Truck and lorry manufacturers are in a difficult position, since the market demands many different body types and small series production is expensive. The solution for this problem is segment design of the cab. Various combinations of the types of cab required can be made up from suitably constructed segments, namely a normal control, forward control or a sleeper cab which can be modified to take extra seats. This design solution is particularly suitable if the cabs are to be used on arrange of vehicles with a common engine.

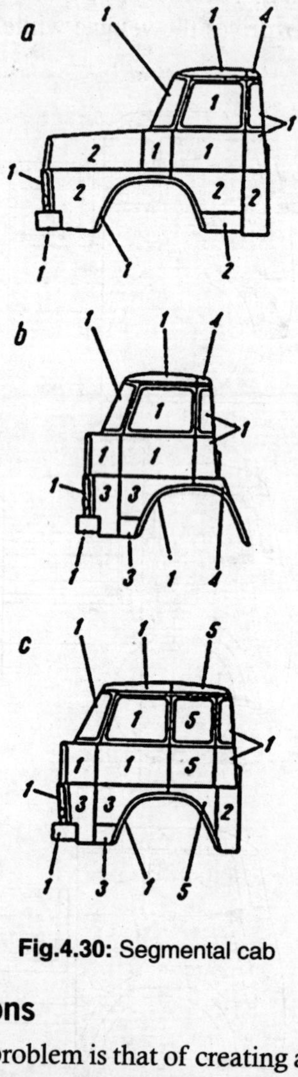

Fig.4.30: Segmental cab

Unification of dimensions

A much more complicated problem is that of creating a cab suitable for vehicles of different loading categories, with quite dissimilar chassis and engines. Unification of dimensions of the driving position (steering wheel, pedals, levers, etc) and also of the chassis frame side members, position of the radiator etc., is necessary. When such unification is achieved, a segment type of cab can be worked out with a common upper part as shown in Fig.4.31. The lower part varies for different types of chassis, taking into consideration the wheel track, engine capacity and so on.

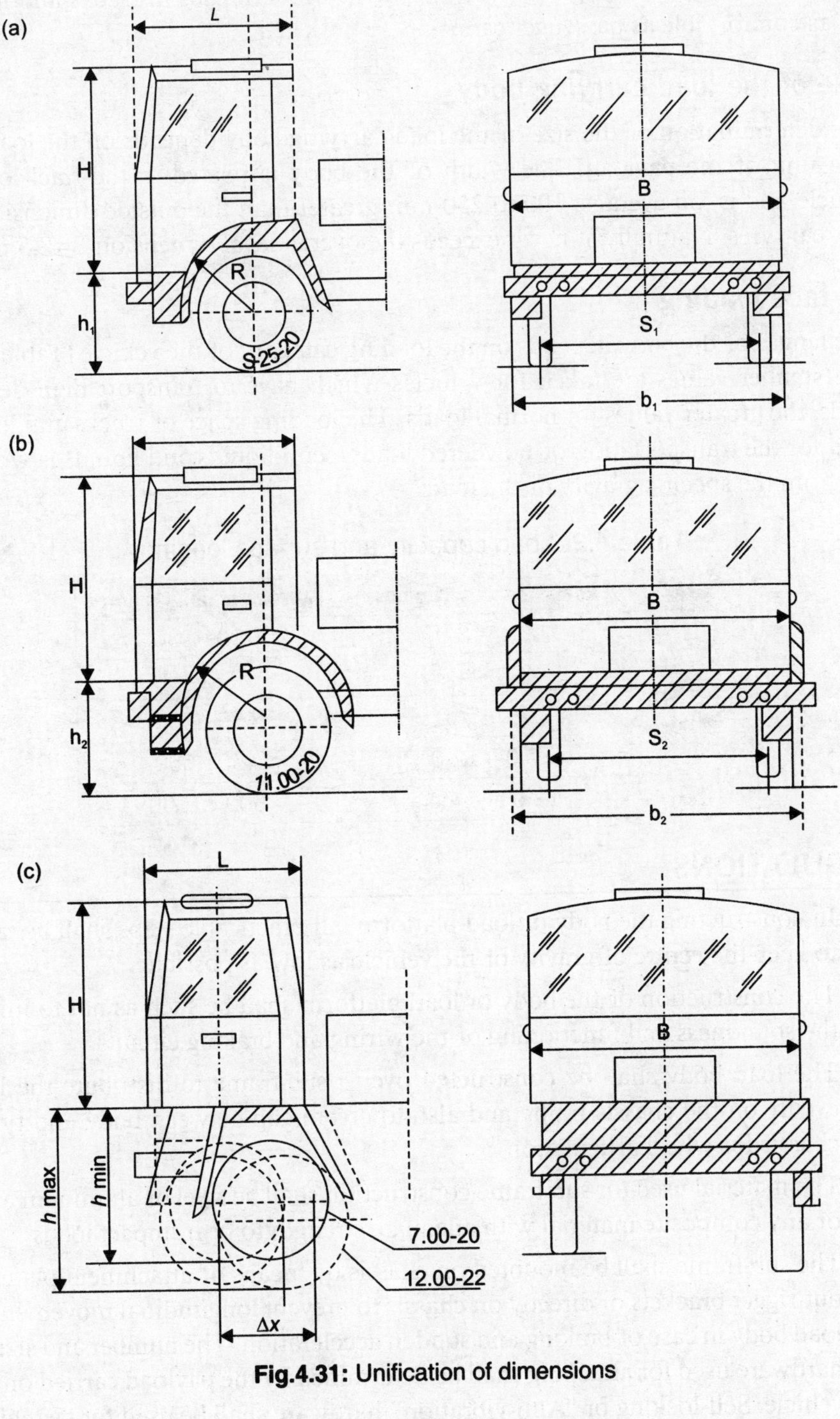

Fig.4.31: Unification of dimensions

Comfort

The design of the cab should ensure a degree of comfort for the crew directly related to the duration of their work inside it. Modern cabs in trucks and lorries are as comfortable as passenger cars.

Size of the load carrying body

The determination of the size of the load-carrying body depends on the load per area unit of the payload. The width of the body is related to the track of the vehicle and is, on average, 100 to 250 mm greater than the outside dimension of the rear tyres. Naturally, it never exceeds the overall legal dimension B=2.5 m.

Surface loading

The length of the body depends on the loading category of the vehicle (Table 4.2). The smaller values are taken for vehicles which have to transport high density loads, the greater values for normal loads. The loading space of trucks and lorries used for the transportation of powdered loads, semi-liquids and liquids is worked out from the specific gravity of the load.

Table 4.2: Load capacity and surface loading

S.No	Load capacity (tonnes)	Surface loading (kg/m²)
1.	0.8 – 2.0	190 - 330
2.	2.0 – 4.0	300 - 450
3.	4.0 – 7.0	450 - 650
4.	7.0 – 12.0	450 - 650
5.	12.0 and more	600 - 1000

REGULATIONS

1. In constructing the body or load platform, all practicable steps shall be taken to keep the centre of gravity of the vehicle as low as possible.
2. The construction of the body or load platform shall be such as not to impair the soundness and functioning of the wiring and braking circuits.
3. The load body shall be constructed over a sub-frame to distribute the load evenly on the chassis frame and also to create gap between body and tyre / chassis for wheel articulation.
4. The material used for sub-frame construction shall be steel or aluminum alloy or any composite material with adequate strength to bear impact loads.
5. The sub-frame shall be mounted on chassis by means of attachment plates or out-rigger brackets or directly on chassis to prevent longitudinal movement of load body in case of braking and sudden acceleration. The number and size of hardware used for attaching shall be determined by the payload carried on the vehicle. Self-locking or "Anti-vibration" hardware shall be used for fastening.

6. The floor, head board (also called crash guard or front wall) and side walls are the main load bearing elements of the body. The floor shall be rigidly supported on the sub-frame. The section of floor and floor supports in the sub-frame shall be pitched / spaced to achieve distributed loads even in case of concentrated loads such as steel coils or forklifts etc.
7. The side walls and crash guard shall be constructed to bear a part of load carried on the vehicle in case of braking, turning, travel on slopes etc. as given below, which can also be proved by FEM analysis.
   - Side walls: 30 % of rated pay load carried.
   - Crash guard or head board: 40% of rated pay load carried, the maximum however being 5000 kgf.
   - Rear wall or tail gate: 25% of rated pay load carried.
8. Where the cab and bodywork are integral, account shall be taken of the flexibility of the cab mounting.
9. In the case of tank-vehicles, where outrigger brackets are used to fasten the tank to the chassis of the vehicle, the vertical face of the brackets shall not be less in height than the depth of the chassis frame to which they are attached.
10. In the case of tipping vehicles, where there is no supplementary underframe, to distribute the load, the pivot brackets for rearward tipping bodies shall be located as near as possible to the rear spring brackets to minimize additional bending stresses on the chassis frame during tipping.
11. In the case of bodies tipping rearwards only, guide plates shall be provided to control the lateral movement of the body when lowered onto the chassis frame.
12. In the case of tipping bodies, steps shall be taken to prevent excessive noise caused by the bodywork of the vehicle when it is unladen.

Review Questions

Short Questions

1. What is a light commercial vehicle?
2. State the different types of tipping mechanism used in tipper body.
3. Draw the layout of the driver's seat of a forward control vehicle.
4. Indicate the seating dimensions for the driver of tanker body.
5. What is meant by tipping mechanism?
6. State the different types of tipping mechanism used in tipper body.
7. State the different examples of commercial vehicle body.
8. List out the factors to be considered for designing a driver's seat.

9. List out the major factors to be considered in a tipper body design.
10. Briefly explain about the segmental design of driver's cab.
11. Mention the different types of commercial vehicle body.
12. What is meant by compactness of driver's cab?
13. Briefly illustrate the compactness of driver's cab with relevant figures.
14. Differentiate a drop side commercial vehicle from that of a fixed side vehicle.
15. How is the load carrying body of a Tipper actuated?

Long Questions

1. Explain the constructional details of a tanker body.
2. Explain the construction of a tipper body with relevant sketch.
3. Explain the design consideration of drivers cab.
4. What are the parameters to be considered in designing the driver's seat?
5. Discuss about light commercial vehicle body with a neat sketch.
6. Explain the classification of LCVs with relevant sketches.
7. Discuss the different types of commercial vehicle body building with illustration.
8. Draw a neat sketch of the following and name the salient parts: (1) Flat platform body (2) Tipper body (3) Tanker body.
9. With a graph illustrate the effect of the inclination of steering column and height of driver's seat on the force exerted by the driver on driving controls.

5 Vehicle Aerodynamics

AERODYNAMICS

Aerodynamics is a branch of physics and is concerned with all the processes which can be observed when air flows around a body. This study deals with a solid body moving through the atmosphere and the interaction which takes place between the body surfaces and the surrounding air with varying relative speeds and wind direction.

Economy is of decisive importance in the transport sector. The most important factors in reducing fuel consumption in long distance traffic with its high average speeds are the economy of the drive train and aerodynamics.

As regards aerodynamics, the following are some of the features incorporated into the vehicle design.

- Large corner radii on the front section
- Low-level front skirts
- Fairings above and behind the driver's cab
- Aerodynamically shaped mirrors
- Enclosed steps

In addition to optimizing the shape of the driver's cab in terms of air flow to improve fuel consumption, there are a number of other aims to be considered in aerodynamic design, namely:

- Intensive air flow around cooling units
- Optimized air flow through the interior of cab
- Minimizing dirt deposition on visible areas
- Reducing impairment of the vision of other drivers in the wet

Importance of aerodynamics

With proper aerodynamic design, the following advantages could be achieved.

1. Drag force is reduced. So maximum speed and acceleration are obtained for the same power output.
2. Fuel consumption of the vehicle can be reduced to the maximum (about 35% of fuel cost).
3. Gives better appearance and styling.
4. By reducing the various forces and moments, good stability and safety can be achieved.
5. Helps to provide proper ventilation system.
6. Helps to understand the dirt flow and exhaust gas flow patterns.
7. Aerodynamic noise could be reduced which results in quite running of the vehicle.

AERODYNAMIC FORCES AND MOMENTS

It is generally true that a car designed with sufficient attention to aerodynamics will be more expensive, but by lowering drag the economy can be improved. Careful attention to the effects of lift, cross wind forces and the three moments result in vehicles which are easier to drive and safer.

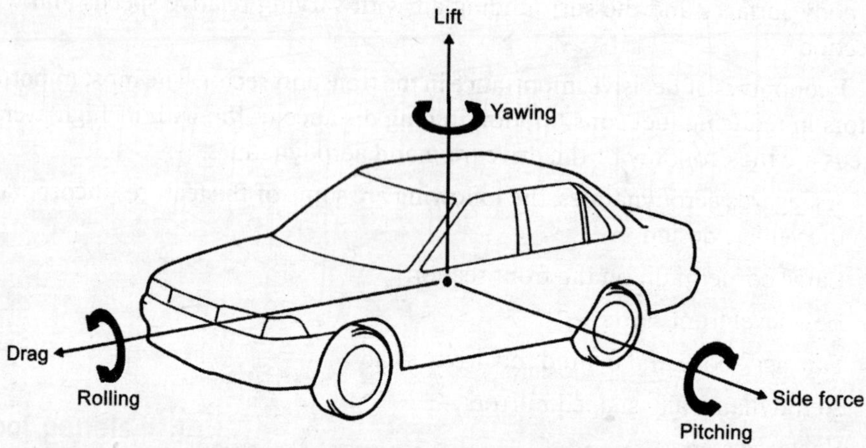

Fig.5.1: Aerodynamic forces and moments

Aerodynamic forces and moments acting on the vehicle are balanced by wheel reactions. In order to analyze the various aerodynamic forces and moments acting on the vehicle body, consider the vehicle as a mass having six degrees of freedom.

Now the various aerodynamic forces acting on the vehicle body can be summarized as follows:

Px – Force of air drag in the direction of motion with wind angle along the longitudinal axis.

Py – Cross wind force

Pz – Aerodynamic lift

Since these forces are not acting at the centre of gravity but at the centre of pressure, they cause moments as follows:

M_y = Pitching moment caused by the forces P_z and P_x about the y axis.

M_z = Yawing moment caused by the force P_y about the z axis.

M_x = Rolling moment caused by the force P_y about the x axis.

AERODYNAMIC FORCES

Aerodynamic drag (Px)

The total aerodynamic drag of a vehicle includes many factors, such as profile drag, induced drag, skin friction, interference drag and cooling and ventilation system drag. The total aerodynamic drag can be written in the usual form:

$$P_x = C_x \rho A v^2 / 2$$

Where,

C_x – Dimensionless drag co-efficient

ρ – Air density in kg/m³

V – Velocity of wind in m/s

A – Cross sectional area of the vehicle viewed from the front, m²

Effects

Aerodynamic drag is proportional to the square of velocity, and hence the power needed to overcome drag is proportional to the cube of velocity. This means that there is a very strong relationship between the speed that a vehicle is travelling and the proportion of the fuel used to overcome drag.

For passenger cars this means that aerodynamics is responsible for a much higher proportion of the fuel used in the highway cycle than the city cycle: 50% for highway; versus 20% for city. This means that if there is 10% reduction in aerodynamic drag, highway fuel economy will improve by approximately 5%, and city fuel economy by approximately 2%.

Cross wind force (Py)

It is formed by the asymmetric flow of air around the vehicle body when the wind angle is not equal to zero. The cross wind force can be given as

$$Py = Cy \rho A v^2 / 2$$

Where,

Cy – Cross wind force dimensionless co-efficient

The values of the cross wind coefficient are shown in Fig.5.2 for different vehicle body shapes. The lowest values of the cross wind force coefficient are obtained with the streamlined bodies of sports cars.

Saloons, vans, and vintage cars have increasingly larger values. The actual values of the cross wind force obtained are indicated in Fig.5.3 and these range from 10 to 15% of the weight of the vehicle.

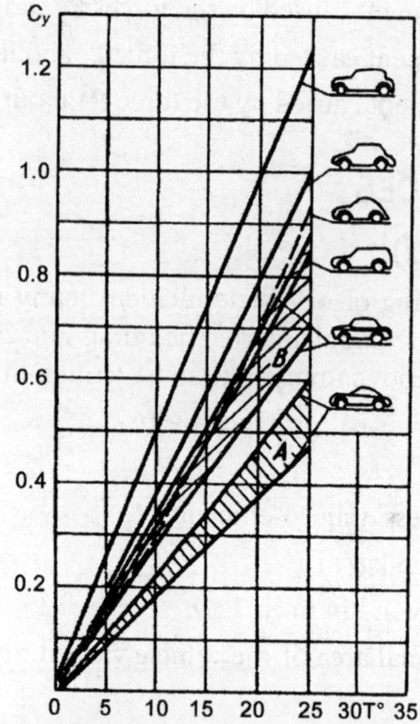

Fig.5.2: Cross wind co-efficient

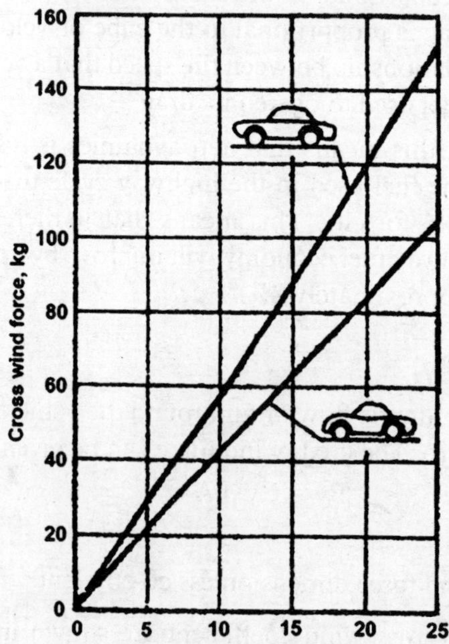

Fig.5.3: Cross wind force for a saloon at 120 km/hr

Effects

Crosswind moves the path of vehicles sideways and can be a hazard.

Aerodynamic lift (Pz)

It is the vertical component of the resultant of the pressure distribution over the vehicle body due to flow of air around it. The aerodynamic lift can be represented as

$$Pz = Cz \rho A v^2 / 2$$

Where,

Cz – Lift co-efficient

Effects

The lift will tend to reduce the pressure between the wheels and the ground, which causes losses of steering on the front axle and the loss of friction on the rear axle. The magnitude of this lift and its distribution over the front and rear is a function of ground clearance, the contours of the body and the under body and the angle of attack of the air on the vehicle body.

AERODYNAMIC MOMENTS

Rolling moment (M_x)

The centre of the aerodynamic forces is usually above the centre of gravity so that the cross wind force P_y will produce a rolling moment M_x about the longitudinal axis. This magnitude of this rolling moment is given by

$$M_x = P_y a = C_{mx} \rho A L v^2 / 2$$

Where,

a – Height of centre of thrust above CG

C_{mx} – Rolling moment coefficient

L – Reference length

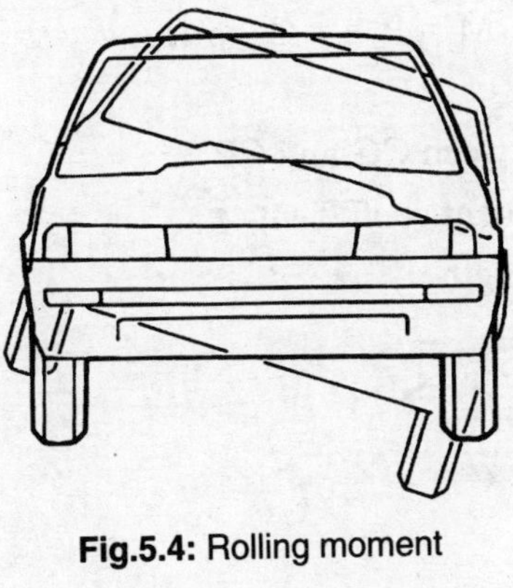

Fig.5.4: Rolling moment

Effects

The rolling moment effects the weight distribution on the wheels. This effect is dangerous for coaches and particularly for tall vans where the side force acts much above the CG. The only solution to reduce rolling moment is to increase the wheel track (wheel tread).

Pitching moment (M_y)

This moment is caused about Y-axis by cross wind force P_y or the longitudinal force P_x. The pitching moment M_y is given by

$$M_y = P_x\, b = C_{my}\, \rho\, A\, L\, v^2 / 2$$

Where,

b – Distance between CG and CP

C_{my} – Pitching moment coefficient

L – Reference length of the wheel base

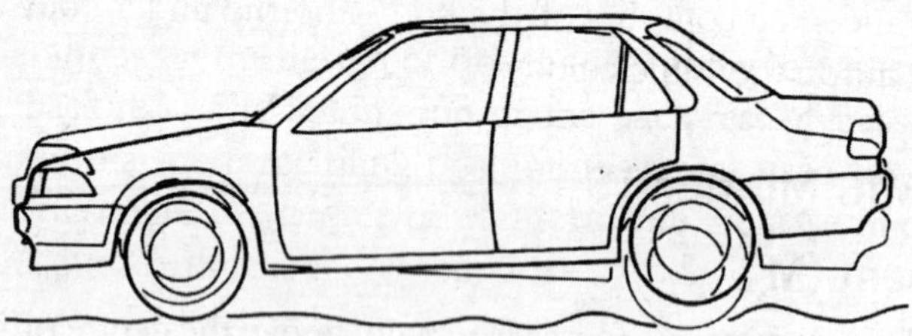

Fig.5.5: Pitching moment

Effects

The pitching moment is usually negative i.e., nose down and this moves. The rear axle lifts off the ground and further reduces the available traction.

Yawing moment (Mz)

This moment is caused about Z-axis by cross wind force P_y. The yawing moment M_z is given by

$$M_z = P_y\, e = C_{mz}\, \rho\, A\, L\, v^2 / 2$$

Where,

e – Distance between CG and CP

C_{mz} – Yawing moment coefficient

L – Reference length

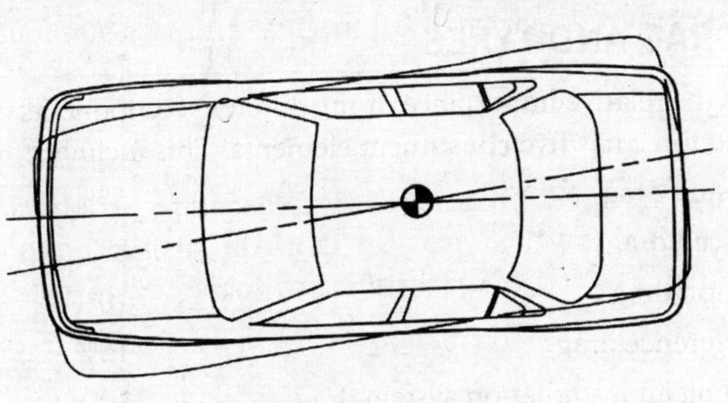

Fig.5.6: Yawing moment

Effects

These moments adversely affects the directional stability of the vehicle at high speed. The use of stabilizer fins at the rear of the vehicle gives a very good reduction in yawing moment.

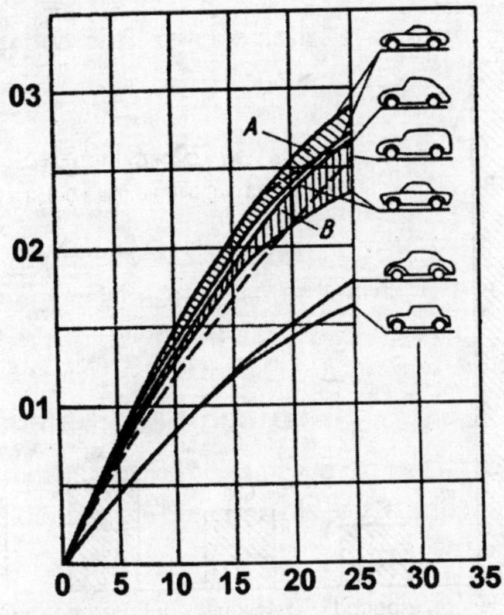

Fig.5.7: Yawing moment coefficients

Fig.5.7 gives values of C_{mz} obtained from wind tunnel tests. It is worthy of note that vehicle bodies with good aerodynamic direct force coefficients (low values of C_x, C_z and C_y) have the largest values of C_{mz}. Therefore, a vehicle with poor aerodynamic properties will have a better (lower) yawing moment coefficient. In addition, all the vehicle bodies illustrated are aerodynamically directionally unstable, because the side wind will produce a yawing moment tending to turn the vehicle away from the direction of motion.

Note:

CG – is the point where the whole mass of a system is assumed to be act.

CP – is the point where the total pressure acts on the system.

VEHICLE DRAG AND TYPES

Fig.5.8 shows the relative importance of the different components of aerodynamic drag. The drag force has five constituent elements. This includes:

a. Pressure drag — 57%
b. Induced drag — 8%
c. Friction drag — 10%
d. Interference drag — 15%
e. Cooling and ventilation system drag — 10%

Profile drag

The profile drag (57%) which depends upon the longitudinal section of the vehicle body plays the most important part. A careful choice of body profile is essential for low drag coefficient; streamlines should be continuous and separation of boundary layer with its attendant vortices should be avoided.

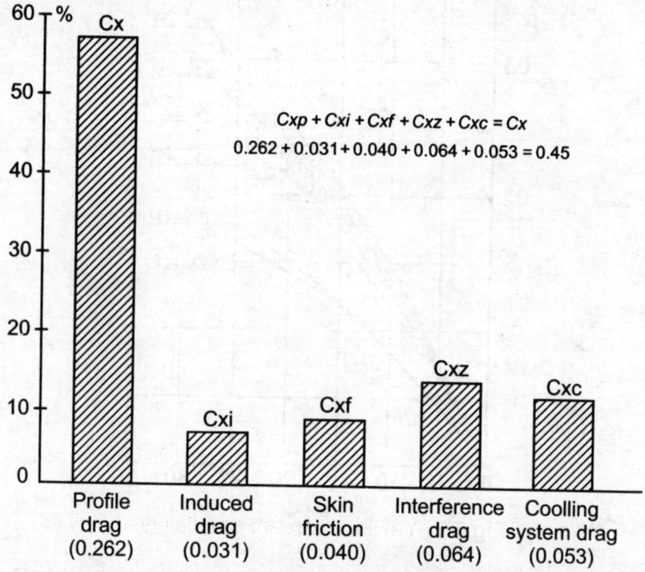

Fig.5.8: Different components of aerodynamic drag

Induced drag

Induced drag (8%) is caused by vortices formed at the side of the vehicle and traveling downwind from it. These vortices are caused by the aerodynamic lift of the vehicle body, and the co-efficient of induced drag (Cxi) is proportional to C^2_z.

Friction drag

Friction drag contributes about 10% of the aerodynamic drag and is caused by the friction force between the boundary layer and the body surface. If this surface is kept smooth, a laminar boundary layer will be maintained further along the vehicle than with a rough surface. Assuming a smooth front to the vehicle, a well polished surface is not only attractive but makes the vehicle more economical.

Interference drag

Interference drag contributes 15% to the total drag. It includes such elements as projecting door handles, mirrors, aerials, and badges which project out of the normal surface of the vehicle body.

Also, projections below the vehicle such as axles, tow-bars, etc., contribute towards the interference drag.

Cooling and ventilation drag

Cooling and ventilation drag contributes 10% of the total drag. With careful attention to the design of ducting in the vehicle, it should be possible to reduce this value considerably for fast vehicles and in theory to use the energy given to the airflow by the radiator to secure a positive forward force or negative drag.

DRAG CO-EFFICIENT (C_D)

The aerodynamic drag coefficient is a measure of the effectiveness of a streamline aerodynamic body shape in reducing the air resistance to the forward motion of a vehicle. Low C_D values indicate low drag and allow a higher terminal speed and lower fuel consumption. A low drag coefficient implies that the streamline shape of the vehicle's body is such as to enable it to move easily through the surrounding viscous air with the minimum of resistance. Conversely a high drag coefficient is caused by poor streamlining of the body profile so that there is a high air resistance when the vehicle is in motion. The drag coefficient is calculated in tests carried out in aerodynamic or wind tunnels. It indicates the magnitude of a vehicle's drag as a result of its shape.

Typical drag coefficients for various classes of vehicles can be seen as follows:

Vehicle type	Drag co-efficient (C_D)
Saloon car	0.22 – 0.40
Sports car	0.28 – 0.40
Light van	0.35 – 0.50
Buses and coaches	0.40 – 0.80
Articulated trucks	0.55 – 0.80
Ridged truck and drawbar trailer	0.70 – 0.90

The drag coefficient of a vehicle can be significantly reduced by rounding the front section and using a front apron, a roof spoiler and side skirts. Only a slight improvement in the drag coefficient is possible by altering the external shape of a commercial vehicle body since rounding the corners and edges reduces the load space and hence the payload. In combination with air deflectors, an aerodynamically optimized cab provides significant reductions in the drag of the vehicle as a whole.

Another measure for reducing resistance is to enclose the exposed running gear of the vehicle with fairings. This reduces the air resistance of the vehicle especially in a cross-wind.

AERODYNAMIC LIFT AND PITCHING MOMENT

The vertical component of the resultant of the pressure distribution is called aerodynamic lift (P_Z). The majority of vehicles have a profile which has the same effect as an aerofoil, with the streamlines over the upper part having a higher velocity than the streamlines below the vehicle.

Aerodynamic lift is applied through the centre of pressure of the body profile and since this point does not correspond with the centre of gravity, it creates a pitching moment about the lateral axis. The aerodynamic lift can be represented by:

$$Pz = Cz\ \rho\ A\ v^2 / 2$$

Where,

- Cz – Lift co-efficient
- ρ – Air density in kg/m^3
- V – Velocity of wind in m/s
- A – Cross sectional area of the vehicle viewed from the front.

Similarly the pitching moment:

$$My = Px\ e = Cmy\ \rho\ A\ L\ v^2 / 2$$

Where,

- b – Distance between CG and CP
- Cmy – Pitching moment coefficient
- L – Reference length. e.g. Wheel base

Effects

Both aerodynamic lift and pitching moment have undesirable effects.

The lift will tend to reduce the pressure between the wheels and the ground, which causes loss of steering on the front axle and loss of traction on the rear axle.

Pitching moment is usually negative, i.e. nose down, and this makes the rear axle lift off the ground and further reduce the available traction.

Effect of fairing on lift and pitching moment

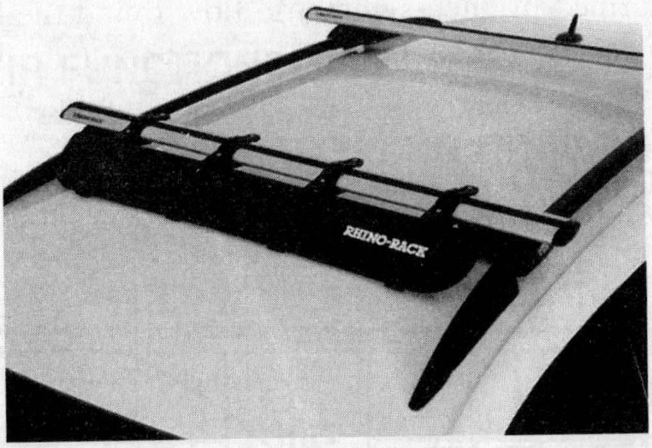

Fig.5.9: Fairing

Fairing is an additional part or structure added to a car to smooth the outline and thus reduce drag.

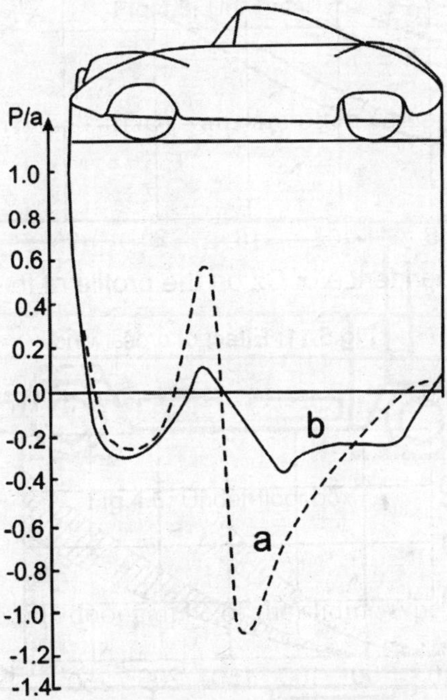

Fig.5.10: Fairing pressure distribution

A typical pressure distribution is shown in Fig.5.10. It can be seen that if a fairing is used to cover the cockpit there will be an increase in both lift and pitching moment. However, if a fairing is not used there will be an advantageous effect on lift and pitching moment but an increase in the drag coefficient. It is also shown that with the fairing fitting, the large area of negative pressure is toward the rear of the car. It is this negative pressure which causes the increase in lift and negative pitching moment.

SIDE WIND EFFECTS ON FORCES AND MOMENTS

Side force P_Y is formed by the asymmetric flow round the body of the vehicle when the wind angle τ is not equal to zero.

EFFECT OF SIDE WIND ON LIFT FORCE

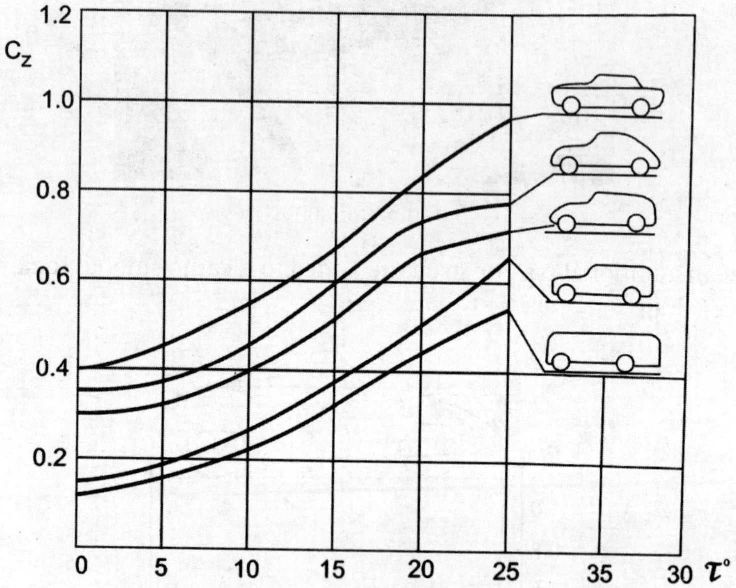

Dependence of Cz on the profile of the vehicle body

Fig.5.11: Effect of cross wind

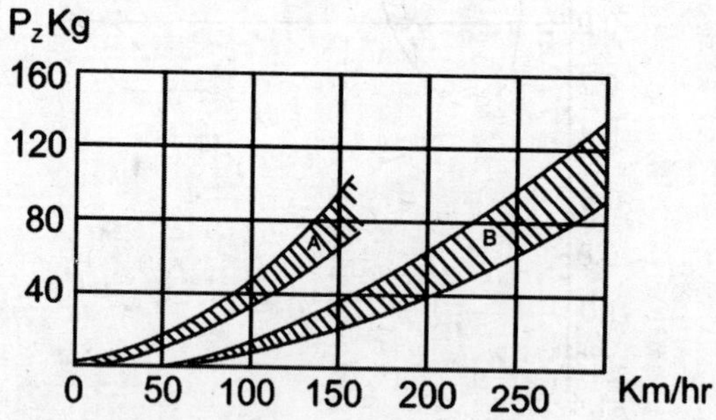

Fig.5.12: Importance of aerodynamic lift

The effect of cross wind as shown in Fig.5.11 indicating that the lift coefficient increases parabolically with the increase in the wind angle, up to 2 or 3 times its value when there is no side wind. Fig.5.11 shows this effect for various vehicle profiles, indicating that the 3-box configuration has the greatest spread of lift coefficients (0.4-1.0) while the flat fronted type of vehicle has the smallest range (0.15-0.55). The importance of aerodynamic lift is shown in Fig.5.12, where the figure for saloon cars can reach a value of 100 kg or 8 to 10% of the total weight.

In the case of sports cars or racing cars the lift can reach values of 130 kg, which is 15 to 25% of the total weight.

EFFECT OF SIDE WIND ON MOMENTS

Side wind force also acts at the centre of pressure and creates moments about the centre of gravity-yawing moment M_Z about the z axis and a rolling moment M_X about the x axis.

Yawing moment

The side wind will produce a yawing moment tending to turn the vehicle away from the direction of motion.

Because of the serious consequences of the loss of directional control, a better relation between the yawing moment coefficient (C_{mz}) and the side wind angle (τ°) is required.

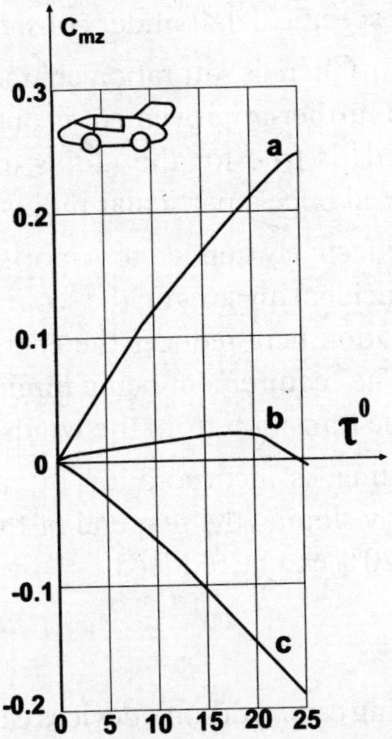

Fig.5.13: Yawing moment coefficients

The use of stabilizers or fins at the rear of the vehicle gives very good results. Without a stabilizer (curve a, Fig.5.13) the vehicle is unstable, while a simple stabilizer (curve b) reduces the yawing moment coefficient and at large cross wind angles, actually provides a stable condition.

Rolling moment

The rolling moment effects the weight distribution on the wheels. This effect is dangerous for coaches and particularly for tall vans where the side force acts much above the CG. The only solution to reduce rolling moment is to increase the wheel track (wheel tread).

VARIOUS BODY OPTIMIZATION TECHNIQUES FOR MINIMUM DRAG

At present three distinct methods are being employed to obtain lower drag co-efficient.

1. Optimisation
2. Add-on devices
3. AB Initio for low drag

OPTIMIZATION

Step-by-step modification of the body details which are important with respect to drag in order to establish a relationship between the drag and the geometrical parameters describing the specific detail under consideration.

After these relationships there is saturation characteristic i.e. beyond a certain value of the parameter no further improvement is obtained and this is then taken as the optimum value. This is true for the radius of leading edges, where floe separation is fully suppressed once a particular radius is exceeded.

Optimisation can be effectively applied to A-ports and the rear edges. Because of their inclination to the incident air stream, the separation at the A-ports takes the form of vortices. Optimization here reduces the energy expanded in the vortices and so reduces the drag. The requirement being minimise the projections such as drip-rails and to smooth the transition from the windscreen to the door glass.

A degree of 'boat-tailing' is incorporation by tapering body sides inwards towards the rear and slightly sloping the rear end of the roof. By this optimisation drag co-efficient of about 20% can be reduced.

ADD-ON DEVICES

To reduce the drag of existing cars \add-on\ devices can be used with considerable effect. The two most successful devices used to reduce drag are front and rear spoilers. The front spoiler or air-flow mounted under the nose of the car, shields the under body contours and projections and so reduces the drag contributions. It also lowers the pressure acting on the rear wall of the engine bay thus giving a further reduction in drag, the rear spoiler which is attached either to the rear of the roof or to the rear upper edge of the trunk, has the effect in both locations of increasing the pressure acting on the back deck area, with a consequent decrease in drag. By these add-on devices, drag reduction of about 25% can be achieved.

AB – INITIO METHOD

By having a sight convex profile from A- post to D- post, reduction of about 0.05 can be achieved. By using a wind screen incorporating greater curvature towards the A- post resulted in a shallower angle over the central portion of the screen. The usual sharp discontinuity in the profile at the A-post was thus completely eliminated and within the associated flow separation is also eliminated. However it is difficult to reproduce this feature on a production vehicle. For instance, the perfect smooth profile from the wind screen to D-post edges would inevitably be comprised to some extent at the junction of glass and the surrounding frames and a result in decrease of drag coefficient of 0.02 might be expected.

WIND TUNNELS

A wind tunnel is a device wherein a stream of air of controlled velocity and uniform flow conditions is made to pass over a scale model of a car on which the forces and moments acting thereon can then be measured.

PRINCIPLE OF OPERATION

- The loads exerted by static air on a moving body are equal to those exerted by moving air on a static body, as long as the relative velocities between the air and the body are the same in both cases.
- For a truly representative wind tunnel experiment, the body must have its true size and the wind must have the speed that the object would have if it was moving.
- These conditions are not always possible. Several scaling laws can be used in order to render representative experiments where the size or airspeed have been scaled.

TYPES OF WIND TUNNELS

Wind tunnels can be classified based on air flow speed in test section and based on shape.

BASED ON FLOW SPEED

Subsonic or low speed wind tunnels

Maximum flow speed in this type of wind tunnels can be 135m/s. Flow speed in wind tunnels is generally preferred in terms of Mach number which comes out to be around 0.4 for this case. This type of wind tunnels is most cost effective due to the simplicity of the design and low wind speed. Generally low speed wind tunnels are found in schools and universities because of low budget.

Transonic wind tunnels

Maximum velocity in test section of transonic wind tunnels can reach up to speed of sound i.e. 340m/s or Mach number of 1. These wind tunnels are very common in aircraft industry as most aircrafts operate around this speed.

Supersonic wind tunnels

Velocity of air in test section of such wind tunnels can be up to Mach 5. This is accomplished using convergent - divergent nozzles. Power requirements for such wind tunnels are very high.

Hypersonic wind tunnels

Wind velocity in test section of such type of wind tunnels can measure between Mach 5 and Mach 15. This is also achieved using convergent - divergent nozzles.

BASED ON SHAPE

Open circuit wind tunnel

This type of wind tunnel is open at both ends. The chances of dirt particles entering with air are more so more honeycombs (mesh to clean incoming air) are required to clean the air. Open type wind tunnels can further be divided into two categories:

a. **Suckdown tunnel:** With the inlet open to atmosphere, axial fan or centrifugal blower is installed after test section. This type of wind tunnels are not preferred because incoming air enters with significant swirl.

b. **Blower tunnel:** A blower is installed at the inlet of wind tunnel which throws the air into wind tunnel. swirl is a problem in this case as well but blower tunnels are much less sensitive to it.

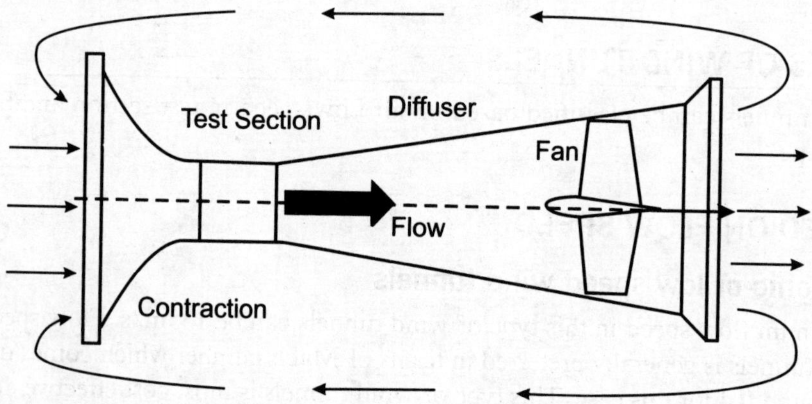

Fig.5.14: Open circuit wind tunnel

Advantages

1. Cheaper to build.

2. Pollutants are purged (e.g. smoke flow visualization or tests on internal combustion engines).

Disadvantages

1. The size of the tunnel must be compatible to the size of the room: the room is the return path for the air.
2. Noisy
3. More expensive to run than closed type.

Closed circuit wind tunnel

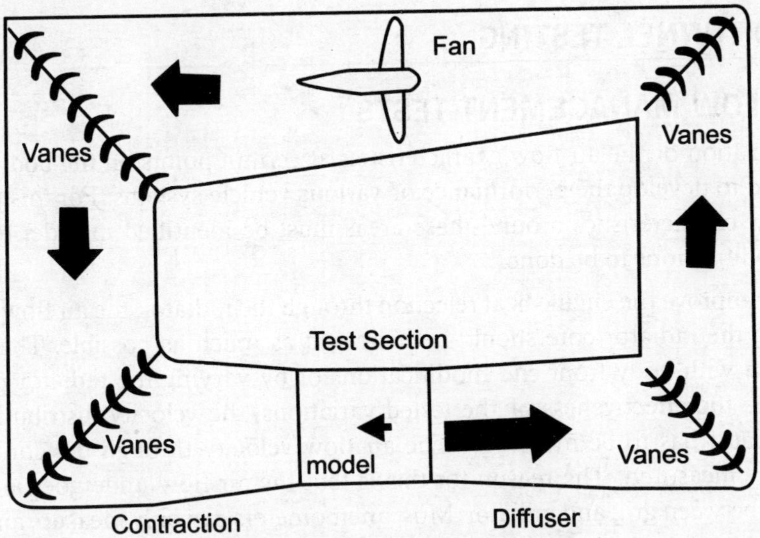

Fig.5.15: Closed circuit wind tunnel

Outlet of such wind tunnel is connected to inlet so the same air circulates in the system in a regulated way. The chances of dirt entering the system are also very low. closed wind tunnels have more uniform flow than open type. This is usually a choice for large wind tunnels as these are more costlier than open type wind tunnels.

Advantages

1. Cheaper to run: energy is required only to overcome losses.
2. Less noisy than open type.
3. The quality of the flow can be easily controlled.

Disadvantages:

1. More expensive to build.
2. Not easy to purge.

3. Continuous losses of energy in the tunnel heat up the air, so the air may need cooling, especially in the summer.

Note:

- Subsonic $0.0 < M < 0.5$
- Subsonic (with mild corrections) $0.5 < M < 0.8$
- Transonic $0.8 < M < 1.2$
- Supersonic $1.2 < M < 3.0$
- High supersonic $3.0 < M < 5.0$
- Hypersonic $5.0 < M$

WIND TUNNEL TESTING

AIR FLOW MANAGEMENT TESTS

Optimization of the air flow characteristics at certain points on the body may be required to develop the performance of various vehicle systems. For this purpose, the flow characteristics around these areas must be identified in order to enable any modifications to be done.

To improve the engine heat rejection through the radiator, the air flow velocity through the radiator core should be increased as much as possible. This can be achieved with body front end modifications or by varying the radiator position. To judge the effectiveness of the tested variations, the velocity distribution over the radiator has to be measured. The air flow velocity through the core cannot be easily measured. The reason for this is that the air flow undergoes a swirling motion between grill and radiator. Most anemometers can only measure air flow in the direction for which they have been set up. The continuously changing direction of air flow around the radiator makes the use of these anemometers questionable. If the measurement is carried out at the rear of the radiator, similar measuring difficulties occur due to turbulence caused by the fan. One possibility however is to use hot wire anemometers, suitable for measurements in three-dimensional flow regimes. These sensors make it possible to determine the air velocity component normal to the core. Moreover, due to their small dimensions, positioning close to the radiator is possible without disturbing the prevailing air flow characteristics. By moving the sensor with a traversing device, continuous tracings of the air velocity distribution across the radiator core can be recorded.

Another air flow measurement task is the optimization of the brake cooling air flow. A quality evaluation of the air flow characteristics can be done by using a smoke generator. A mirror positioned beneath the brake assembly enables the observation of the air flow patterns to be made easily. Furthermore, the air velocity distribution in the area in question can be measured using a hot wire anemometer.

A brake cooling performance test delivers quicker information if the wind tunnel is equipped with a dynamometer facility capable of applying a motoring torque. Using the dynamometer, braking is applied at a representative driving speed (example, 100 km/h) to heat up the brake system. Typical temperatures (example, brake fluid, brake disc or drum) are measured. After reading a temperature level representative of severe braking on the road, the brake force is released and the braking system is subjected to tunnel wind until all components have cooled down. The time needed to achieve a selected lower temperature level can be taken as a representative figure to assess the effective cooling capability of the brake assembly. The effectiveness of different measures to improve brake cooling performance can be investigated by performing successive cooling tests.

FLOW VISUALIZATION TECHNIQUES

Visualization of the flow on the vehicle body, the spatial flow close to the vehicle and the air flow pattern in the passenger compartment is an effective method of investigating and understanding the flow field in and around the vehicle.

Wool tufts

The flow patterns adjacent to the vehicle body surface can easily be made visible by using wool tufts and the regions of attached and separated flow can thus be clearly detected.

Tufts can be glued to the surface of the vehicle body model to indicate flow direction. When the tufts stay parallel to the surface and not moved, this usually indicates attached flow. When the flow is separated, the tufts will oscillate violently to all directions. This method can be used for off body visualization by using rakes, or arrays of thin wires to which the tufts are attached, and then placing them in the area of interest.

Oil film method

Another method for surface flow visualization is the application of a surface oil film containing coloured or luminescent pigments. However, attention should be paid to the air flow separation regions because these regions are not always clearly indicated by the oil film method.

Smoke generator

The visualization of spatial flow near to the vehicle body helps significantly in understanding and interpreting the aerodynamic effects of interesting body areas and contours. The most widely used tool for this is a smoke generator. Emitting smoke into the airflow enables the flow patterns to be made visible. The smoke generators most widely used are based on heating a mineral oil derivative until evaporation occurs and a dense white inoffensive smoke is provided. The smoke is then injected into the airflow with the aid of a long thin stem.

A further application of smoke generators is the filling of the separation bubbles and wake zones with smoke to illustrate their form and size. In this case the smoke has to be injected directly into the bubble or wake to fill them.

Helium filled soap bubbles

Similar to smoke, small helium filled soap bubbles are injected into the air flow and their paths are photographed. The buoyancy due to the helium filling is supposed to counteract the water weight and result in zero total buoyancy. The light source can be arranged so that it reflects from the bubbles, highlighting the streamlines in the flow. This technique is especially suitable for flow visualization during small-scale wind tunnel testing.

Particle Image Velocimetry

Particle Image Velocimetry (PIV) is an attractive method for flow visualization, and the main advantage is that quite large areas can be covered. Also, post processing is similar to the post processing of CFD results.

MEASUREMENT OF VARIOUS FORCES AND MOMENTS BY USING WIND TUNNEL

The aerodynamic forces and moments are measured in a wind tunnel using a wind tunnel balance. This is a stationary high-precision measuring instrument. The aerodynamic force and moment figures obtained are then used to calculate the aerodynamic force and moment coefficients.

WIND TUNNEL BALANCES

A wind tunnel balance measures three aerodynamic force components in the x, y and z directions and three aerodynamic moment components tending to rotate the vehicle body about the x, y and z axes of the reference axis system. If the aerodynamic yaw angle is zero, the measurement of only three components is sufficient, namely the force components in the x and z directions and the moment about the y-axis. Hence, for tests at 'straight ahead' position only, a balance of simpler design can be used.

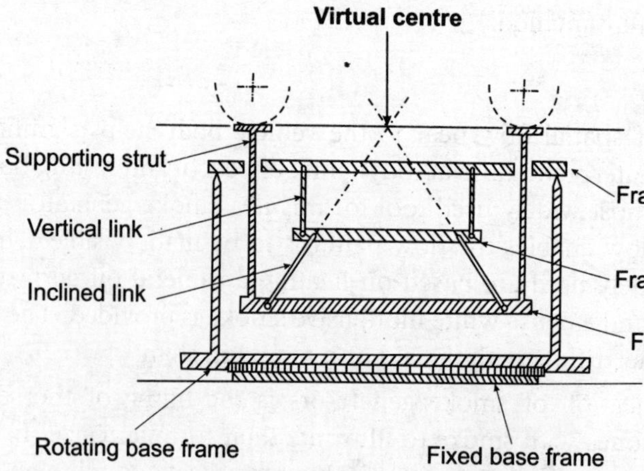

Fig.5.16: Wind tunnel balance

To enable precise force and moment measurements to be made, the wind tunnel balances have to satisfy a number of requirements:

- The balance equipment should not disturb the air flow near the test vehicle. If a support system has to be used (example, during small-scale wind tunnel tests) the influence of this system on the test results has to be determined for subsequent elimination.
- No changes in vehicle set-up position should occur during the measuring procedure.
- The lift forces to be measured are only fractional compared with the initial wheel loads. Hence for accuracy, tare weights have to be used to compensate the pre-loading in the z-direction.
- If the tests are to be carried out at varying yaw angles, provision must be made for the yawing of the balance equipment up to a desired maximum yaw angle.
- Friction and hysteresis must be kept to a minimum in the force transmission mechanisms between the test object and the load sensing systems. The use of special precision components such as knife edge and groove combinations, elastic hinges, hydrostatic and pneumatic bearings, etc., is therefore essential.

Review Questions

Short Questions

1. What are the objectives of vehicle aerodynamics?
2. Define drag force.
3. What are the various drag forces that act on vehicle body?
4. What are different flow visualization techniques?
5. How do you optimize the front end of vehicle for minimum drag?
6. How does the rolling moment caused?
7. Define the term yawing.
8. What are the initial tests that are being carried out in a prototype model?
9. Give the classification of wind tunnel based on the application.
10. List out the various forms of drag.

Long Questions

1. Explain the various forces and moments that act on a vehicle body.
2. Discuss the various types of drag force and its contribution towards the overall drag force.
3. Explain the constructional and operational details of wind tunnel.

4. Explain the various body optimization techniques for minimum drag.
5. Explain how optimization technique can be carried out to reduce the drag due to forehead and windscreen of a car.
6. What is meant by wind tunnel? Explain the classification of a wind tunnel.
7. Explain the principle of operation and types of wind tunnels test.
8. Explain the construction and working of a low speed wind tunnel with a neat sketch.
9. Explain the effect and control of lift, rolling moment and pitching moment on vehicle body design.
10. Explain how aerodynamic drag coefficients can be calculated using a wind tunnel.

6 Body Materials, Trim, Mechanisms and Body Repair

MATERIALS USED IN BODY CONSTRUCTION

All vehicles bodies can be divided into four groups according to the materials used, i.e. metal, wood, plastics or mixed construction.

STEEL SHEET

Sheet steel, ranging in thickness from 0.8 mm to 1.5 mm, is the material most frequently used in vehicle body construction. The introduction of spot-welding for joining sheet metal has made assembly very cheap and suitable for mass-production.

Production process

Steel sheets are usually obtained in rolls from hot-rolling process. After hot rolling, sheets undergo a pickling process to remove the iron oxides or scale from the sheet surface. Scale is a poor electric conductor and prevent spot-welding.

After picking, the sheets are cold rolled. The smoothness of the sheet surface is determined by the number of passes.

Properties

1. This is a low carbon steel with an average carbon content of 0.8% and it is, therefore, a good welding material.
2. Specific gravity is 7.8.
3. The phosphorus and sulphur contaminations are 0.04% and 0.045%.
4. Copper or nickel and chrome are often added to improve the anti-corrosive properties of the sheet metal.
5. The tensile strength, shear strength and elongation of thin steel sheets are given in Table.

Table 6.1: Tensile strength, shear strength and elongation of steel sheets

Process	Tensile strength N/mm²	Shear strength N/mm²	Elongation %
Very deep pressing	280-400	190	28-29
Deep pressing	280-420	200	27-28
Pressing	280-420	200	25-26

ALUMINIUM ALLOY

Sheet aluminium alloy is more expensive but is frequently used for buses and coaches applications both as casting and as sheet metal. It is still economic to use aluminium in this application, as light weight and inherent corrosion resistance offset the higher cost of the material and the more expensive manufacturing methods.

Welding lowers the strength of the material and this type of joint is therefore confined to lightly loaded parts while rivets are used for joining panels which are heavily loaded.

Properties

1. Copper, magnesium, nickel and silicon are added to aluminium to obtain aluminium alloy.
2. The mechanical properties of aluminium alloys depend on heat treatment and ageing.
3. The specific gravity of aluminium alloy is 2.7.
4. Aluminium alloys used for castings and sheet metal working can be welded using a special flux.

TIMBER (WOOD)

Present designs very rarely make use of wooden-framed coachwork. Before the introduction of plastics, wood was used in various ways.

Soft wood

Soft woods such as pine, spruce, etc were used for floor boards and the load containing bodywork of lorries.

Semi-hard wood

Semi-hard woods such as ash and beech were used for body framework.

Hard-wood

Hard woods such as oak, chestnut, etc were used for structural elements having a complicated shape.

Special species of timber such as walnut, acacia, mahogany, etc are used for dashboard finishes in luxury vehicles. Soft-wood fibreboards, plywood and various resin laminated papers are used instead of timber, even for uses such as the floorboards of commercial vehicles.

Drawbacks of wood

Wood has been eliminated as a basic material because of its,

1. High cost
2. High labour cost
3. Short life
4. Heavy

PLASTICS

Generally plastics can be divided into:

1. those obtained from large organic molecules
2. those from condensation polymerisation processes.
3. those from addition polymerisation processes.

PLASTICS FROM LARGE ORGANIC MOLECULES

Celluloid

Plastics from large organic molecules are cellulose-nitrate commonly known as celluloid. Celluloid is used in vehicle body works for decorative linings, anti-glare gazing, various knobs, steering wheel facings, etc. Other materials based on cellulose are cellulose acetate and cellulose butyrate. These are more expensive than cellulose nitrate.

Properties

1. Celluloid with the addition of pigmentations has a very attractive finish.
2. It also possesses good mechanical properties, such as high tensile and impact strength.
3. The main disadvantage of cellulose nitrate is its high inflammability. Cellulose acetate and cellulose butyrate are non-inflammable.

PLASTICS FROM CONDENSATION POLYMERI-SATION PROCESSES

Bakelite

The most important group of plastics obtained from condensation polymerisation is the phenol-plasts, also known as Bakelite. Depending on the polymerisation process, a material suitable for casting or moulding can be obtained.

Cast phenolic resins

Cast phenolic resins are insensitive to temperature and humidity changes, with good dimensional stability and surface finish. Therefore these materials are suitable in the manufacture of control standard pieces for checking the dimensions and shape of body drawpieces.

Cast resins are used as the outer surface for dies and moulds. The core is then filled plastic foams, concrete or even wood. This system saves a large amount of time and expense when compared with metal dies, which require cutting and finishing.

Phenolic resins can also be compounded with a variety of fillers and then used as a moulding material suitable for applications in such body element drawpieces as dashboards, window frames, etc. The addition of wood flour or cotton linters as fillers improves the quality of the material, which can then be used for body panels. Laminations using phenolic resins can be used for roof linings. The technological disadvantages of these materials are that they require hot compression moulding and can only be obtained in dark colours.

Amino resins are obtained from the condensation polymerisation of urea or melamine together with formaldehyde, and are used in vehicle bodies as moulded knobs, grips, plates, etc. Laminates using these resins with paper can be used as floor and wall linings, particularly in food vans, where they can be easily washed down with water. These materials are available in very light pasted colours and even white.

Epoxy resins and phenoplasts have become widely used as materials for dies, moulds and many types of body templates. An additional advantage of using epoxy resins is the possibility of modifying their properties by the addition of fillers such as clay or silica flour. Putties based on epoxy and aluminium power are successfully used for the repair of damaged metal vehicles. This is very useful to designers testing prototypes, in the event of body damage.

PLASTICS FROM ADDITION POLYMERISATION PROCESSES

Plastics obtained by addition polymerisation have wide application in the construction of vehicle bodies.

Poythene and polystyrene

Poythene and polystyrene are used in many types of films and battery cases, and for many other components where metal would be an unsuitable material. These types of plastics are very economical because of their weight to volume ratio, many having densities around 1.00 g/cm^3. Expanded polystyrene can be used as thermo or acoustic insulating boards with densities as low as 0.05 g/cm^3.

Polyvinyl-chloride (PVC)

Another popular product of addition polymerisation is polyvinyl-chloride (PVC).

Rigid PVC is used in vehicle bodies as coatings for such parts as door handles, whilst flexible PVC finds wide use as films, upholstery covering and the roofing in convertibles. It can also be obtained as foam with certain properties superior to those found with rubber foams. The specific gravity of PVC is 1.20-1.60.

Polyester resins

The widely used group of plastics used in the manufacture of car bodies is the polyester resins, which have a specific gravity of 1.5-1.8. Very good mechanical properties are obtained by reinforcing these resins with glass fibres. The fibres are about 0.025 mm in diameter and have a tensile strength of 2500 N/cm^2 and a bending strength of 40000 N/cm^2. The mechanical strength of these composite materials depends on the direction of the fibres and it is important that the fibres are randomly oriented to ensure uniform strength properties.

Polyester resins are simple to mould since they harden at room temperature under normal pressure. This has made for the easy production of whole vehicle bodies. All that is required is a wooden, plaster or plastic model of the body. The surface of this model or mould is treated with a suitable release agent and then the resin and glass fibres are applied to the mould either by hand (using brushes and rollers) or by means of spraying. Sufficient layers are built up to give the desired thickness and then allowed to harden, after which an exact replies is removed from the model.

The only disadvantage of polyester resin is the high cost of the material and the large amount of manual labour required for manufacture.

MIXED CONSTRUCTION

The combination most frequently used is a metal chassis or a complete metal frame work with fibreglass panels. Wood has been used for these outside panels but it has fallen out of use for this purpose and it is only found today in commercial vehicle bodies and here largely as floor covering.

GLASS REINFORCED PLASTIC (GRP)

Glass Reinforced Plastic (GRP) is cheap and easier to work than sheet metal. These were ideal characteristics for the building of prototypes and low volume production cars.

Advantages

- Lightweight
- Does not rust
- Does not get dents

Disadvantages

- Breaks/cracks if bent too much
- Is not as durable as metal
- Can deform with heat

TEXTILES

Cotton-based fabrics are the traditional materials used for the internal trim of a vehicle. The life of this material is short and it also absorbs dust and other impurities. It is now replaced by plastics, of which the most popular are imitation leathers. These consist of soft polyvinylchloride attached to a cotton fabric base. Modern imitation leathers have a quality and appearance as good as leather and are more durable. PVC fabrics made from woven polyester fibres are better than imitation leather. These are cheap and are available in different colours.

GLASS

The glass used for windows in vehicle bodies has a specific gravity of 3.5. Safety glass must be used in vehicle body structures so that injury will not be caused to passengers in the event of breakage.

Toughened glass

Toughened glasses must be used in vehicle body structures so that injury will not be caused to the passengers in the event of breakage. It disintegrates into small pieces with blunt edges.

Laminated glass

Toughened glass cannot be worked after toughening. It cannot be cut or drilled. This disadvantage does not apply to laminated glass where layers of ordinary glass are glued together with a transparent foil which prevents splintering when breakage occurs.

Transparent plastics

Transparent plastics made from polymethyl methacrylate are used in body construction.

1. It is lighter in weight and having a specific gravity only half that of silicic glass.
2. It has good mechanical properties such as tensile strength of 7000 N/cm^2, bending strength of 14000 N/cm^2 and compressive strength of 11500 N/cm^2. Because of its above mechanical properties, transparent plastics can be used as stress carrying members in the bodywork. They can be riveted to the rest of the structure.

3. They have excellent transparency and can be dyed to many shades.
4. By adding the appropriate constituents it is possible to make this type of glass resistant to infra-red rays in order to maintain a low temperature within the vehicle.
5. Its usage in touring coaches enables the passengers to acquire ultra-violet rays from sun while traveling.
6. A minor disadvantage is the ease with which the surface can be scratched, but this is compensated by the fact that it is easily polished.
7. The temperature at which the transparent plastic softens is about 100°C. It makes the moulding of the plastic very easy.

RUBBERS

Synthetic rubber

Synthetic rubber rather than natural rubber is used in vehicle body structures. Synthetic rubber is resistant to fuel oil and can, therefore, be used near petrol tanks and in the engine compartment.

Foam rubber

Foam rubbers are used in bodywork and are divided into the closed and open cell types. The closed cell type does not absorb water and is, therefore, used for outside sealing. Open cell rubber is used for seat cushions and other soft furnishings inside the body.

The hardness of rubber is measured in international rubber hardness degrees, for instance, 30 degrees International Rubber Hardness Density (IRHD) indicates a very soft rubber and 100 degrees IRHD is the hardest rubber in use. For glass sealing, etc., very soft rubbers are used and these closed cell materials have a hardness of well below 30 degrees IRHD. The specific gravity of cellular rubber is a function of the size of the air cells contained within it and is usually within the limit of 0.9 to 1.9.

INSULATING MATERIALS

A low-coefficient of thermo-conductivity and a high coefficient of vibration damping are required for insulating materials. These coefficients are difficult to obtain simultaneously in any one material. Good thermal insulation properties can be obtained in materials which have included air bubbles but these make the materials non-elastic. Elasticity is a necessary condition for vibration damping. In this situation, there are two possibilities:

1. The use of materials, one has the damping qualities and the other provides thermal insulation (second is placed on the top of the first).
2. The use of material with compromise properties.

Cork

Sheets of expanded cork are the oldest material used for heat insulation. It has a specific gravity of 0.15.

Plastics

Expanded polystyrene (plastics) with a specific gravity of 0.04 is lighter, cheaper and have better insulating properties.

Several other plastics have the better thermal and acoustic properties and also protect against corrosion. Some of these plastics are:

- Urea formaldehyde, with specific gravity of 0.03 to 0.04.
- Polyurethene, with specific gravity of 0.05 to 0.06; neoprene with specific gravity of 0.05 to 0.07.

All these materials foam and harden more quickly after spraying if they are heated to about 50°C. Their thermo-acoustic effectiveness depends on the thickness of the layer. By increasing the foaming process, better thermal insulation can be created since larger bubbles are included. Conversely better sound damping properties can be obtained by reducing the degree of foaming.

Felt

Felt is used extensively as an acoustic insulator. The most popular are spraying compounds having an asphalt base with asbestos fibres added. It is necessary to use these compounds in all vehicle bodies near sources of noise such as floor panels and other large surfaces.

BODY TRIM ITEMS

Car trim refers to all the 'decorative' parts that do not add functionality to the vehicle while enhancing the aesthetic and 'cool factor'.

In general, all items that are added to the body structure are called trim items. Seat cushions, instruments, floor coverings, accessories such as ventilation and air conditioning systems, moldings, floor linings, head linings, door locks, handles, arm rests, windshield, window winding mechanisms, lights, and mirrors, glasses, etc are called trim items. It can be divided into interior trim and exterior trim.

The 'soft trims' are the group of parts comprising the seats, carpets, head lining, and the inner trim panels fitted to doors and rear quarters.

EXTERIOR TRIM

Exterior trim can make the car more beautiful and fashionable and meet people's demanding meets about aesthetic and individual needs. Automotive solar films decoration, body film, install body kit, plate and the spoiler, skylight, decorative lights, side-skirt and also the bumpers can be considered trims.

Door hinges

In the modern metal-framed bodywork and doors, the hinge consists of a piece of flat plate, curved to shape, one end which is rigidly fixed to the door, and the other end having an eye for the hinge pin.

INTERIOR TRIM

Everything that is not moving, not displaying info, and is not there for functional reason can be considered an interior trim. Interior trim changes inner appearance and create a warm, comfortable interior environment. Leather steering wheel, car roof lining decoration, door liner, liner decorative side panels, floor coverings, seat trim, interior wood trim, dashboard decoration, interior decoration accessories, sun visor mirror and so on.

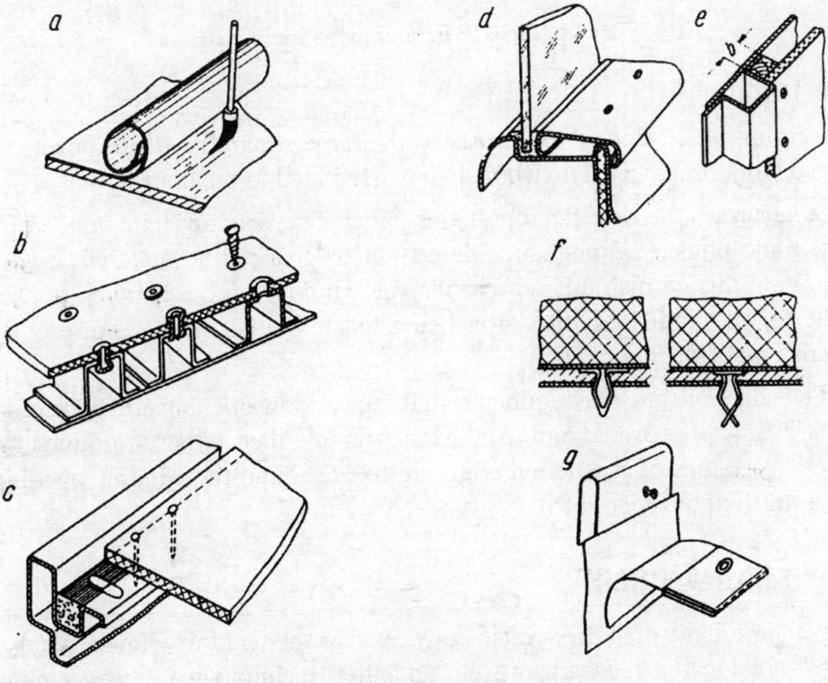

Fig.6.1: Methods of fixing internal trim

The aesthetic character of the inside of the vehicle is determined largely by the trim of the interior surface. Light colours give the impression of a large vehicle, while dark colours make it appear smaller. Plastics have now completely replaced cloth, leather and wood as the main materials for interior trim. Fig.6.1 shows methods of attaching interior trim. These fixings must be simple and quick to install and must not come loose with use. For fixing the roof lining and other non-rigid trim, mouldings, frames, etc can be used. Such non-rigid trim materials are expensive and time-consuming to install during production, and for these reasons many cheap cars have a minimum of lining materials.

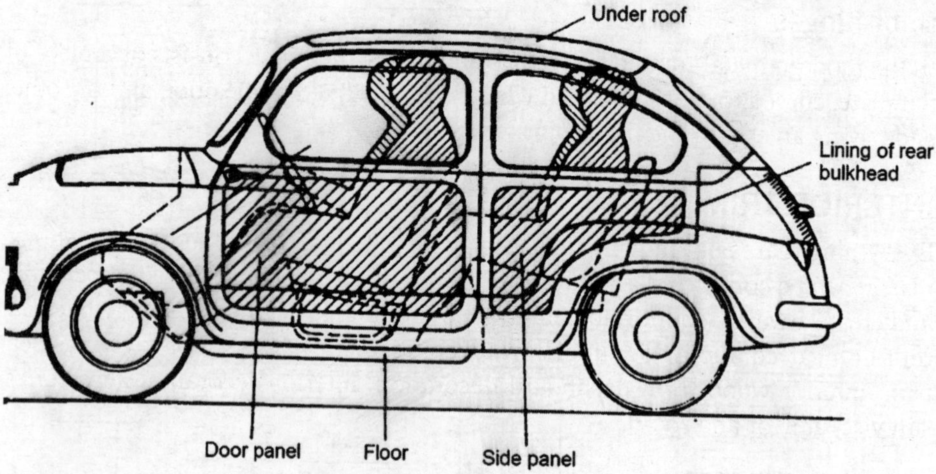

Fig.6.2: Interior trim area

Door triming

The triming of a saloor door consists of a large square of board covered with selected cloth or leather. The whole being assembled to the door frame.

A garnish rail covers the top of this panel. The window being made of well-grained and polished timber such as walnut or of a plastic material. Below the window on this garnish rail is a carrier, the window winder handles, and inside handle for the door lock, the latter being located either in the centre or at the opening end of the door.

The edges of the door triming around the window opening are made of string of board, suitably covered and fixed to the frame. Fillets either of grained timber or metal pressings of plastic material, are fixed around the window openings or form a finish to the edges of the triming.

BODY MECHANISMS

The basic mechanism in the vehicle body, such as the window winder, windshield wiper, door locking mechanisms, etc and their technological advancement are explained in the this topic.

WINDOW WINDER

HAND-CRANK WINDOW

In hand-crank window, turning the winding handle rotates the two parallel links which move the window carrier up and down squarely and smoothly.

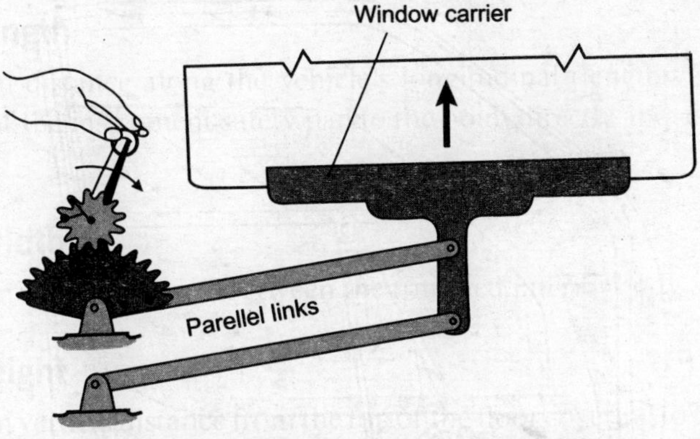

Fig.6.3: Hand-crank window mechanism

POWER WINDOW

Power windows are electric windows which can be raised and lowered at the touch of a button rather than the traditional handle which has to be turned manually for raising and lowering car windows. Power windows are now common on most vehicles. A car with power window is slightly higher in price as compared to the car with normal windows.

Mechanism

Force is transmitted from the motor to the window glass will vary by manufacturer and vehicle model. They will usually comprise a gearbox and scissor-acting lever mechanism. Alternatively a flexible rack or cable assembly can be used as shown in Figs.6.4 and 6.5.

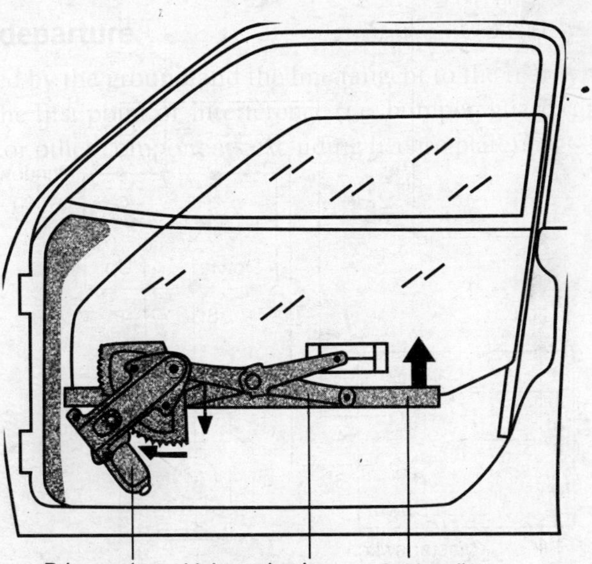

Fig.6.4: Scissor-acting lever mechanism

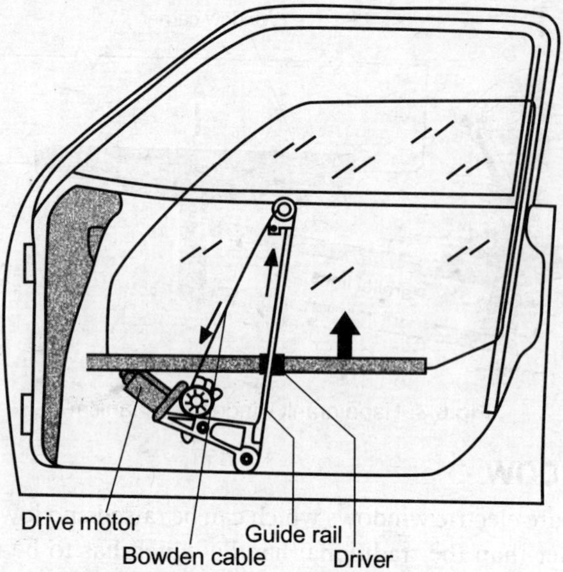

Fig.6.5: Bowden cable mechanism

Working of power windows

Power windows work only when the car is on start mode. When the switch is activated it completes a circuit, sending electricity to the motor which then moves the window up or down.

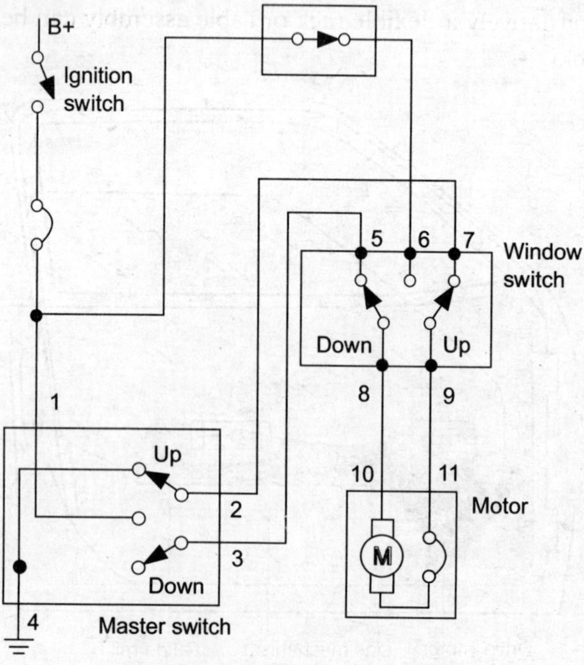

Fig.6.6: Circuit of power window

The motors are controlled by individual switches at each window or by a master switch, usually located on the driver's door. Power for the individual switches is distributed by the master switch. The two switches are wired in series, so a problem with either of them will prevent the window from operating.

The electrical circuit of power window is shown in Fig.6.6. Most systems use permanent-magnet DC motors. These motors can be driven in either direction, depending on the polarity of the wires to the motor. Battery power is supplied to the center of a double-pole, double-throw switch. To operate the window, battery positive power is directed through the motor from the center terminal and flows back to ground through the other side of the switch. Moving the switch in the other direction reverses the polarity of the motor to move the window in the opposite direction. The motor is not grounded to the door but receives its ground through a connection at the master switch.

WINDSHIELD WIPER (SCREEN WIPER)

The windshield wipers are important safety-related features installed to ensure that the driver's view remains unobstructed by wiping off rainwater, snow, bugs, mud, oil, grease from the windshield. It is frequently used in combination with the washer for cleaning off dirt from the windshield glass.

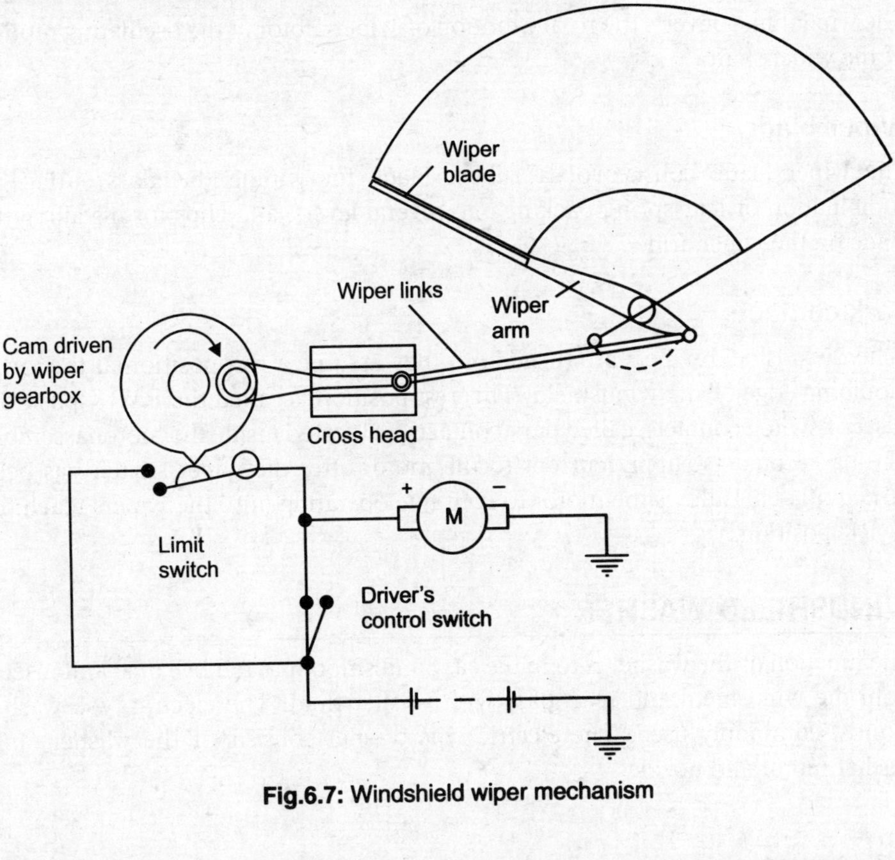

Fig.6.7: Windshield wiper mechanism

The wiper consists of a wiper motor, a wiper link to transmit the driving power, a wiper arm and the wiper blades for the actual wiping.

Most vehicles have two wiper arms for the windshield. Some have an additional wiper for the rear window. Windshield wipers are operated by a wiper switch (controlled by the driver), a wiper motor and a mechanism which links the motor to the wiper arms. Wiper switches can be mounted on the dash board or on the steering column. The wiper mechanism includes a gear reduction unit at the motor. A crank and linkage connect to the wiper arms and convert the rotary motion of the motor into back and forth movement of the wiper arms.

Wiper motor

Most windshield wiper motors are two-speed electric motors with permanent field magnets.

Wiper arm

Wiper arms are mechanical arms, which sweep back and forth across the windshield to remove water, snow, or dirt. The wiper arms have rubber blades, which contact the windshield.

Wiper link

The wiper link converts the rotary motion of wiper motor to the oscillating motion of the wiper shaft.

Wiper blade

The wiper blade consists of a rubber blade for wiping the glass surface, a combination of leaf spring packing and several levers, and clips for installing the blade on the wiper arm.

Park contacts

When windshield wipers are turned off, they assume a rest position at the lower moulding edge of the windshield. This rest position is called the PARK position. A set of switch contacts, called park contacts, is located inside the motor assembly. The park contacts supply current to the motor after the wiper switch has been turned off. This allows the motor to continue operating until the wipers reach the PARK position.

WINDSHIELD WASHER

The function of the washer is to make easy and smooth to remove dust and insects from the windshield and rear glass with washer fluid. The electric type washer is most commonly used. The electric type washer consists of the washer tank, washer motor and nozzles.

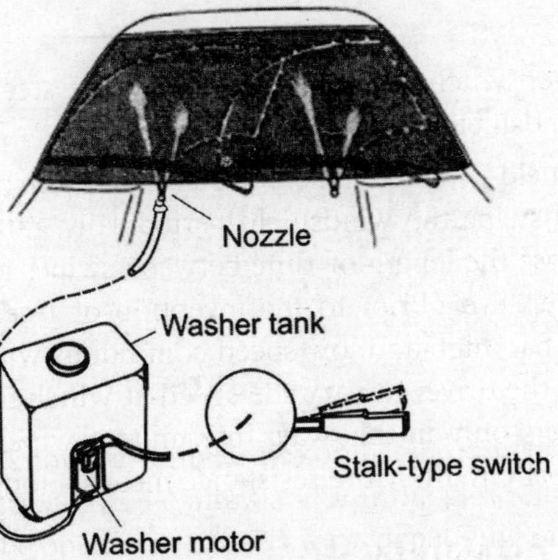

Fig.6.8: Windshield washer

Washer tank

The shape of the washer tank varies depending on the mounting position and available space.

Washer motor (Pump)

The washer motor drives the pump, discharging washer fluid from the tank.

There are several types of pump are used:

1. Gear type
2. Squeeze type
3. Centrifugal type

The centrifugal type is widely used because of its durability due to the use of fewer contacting parts. Since the centrifugal type is only capable of sending the washer fluid to the washers, but is not capable of drawing the fluid up from the tank, it is installed below the washer tank.

Nozzles

The nozzle is made of a copper, aluminium or resin pipe with one or two orifices. At present, resin nozzles fitted with adjustable orifices are most commonly used.

The orifice is 0.8 – 1.0 mm in diameter and one or two in number. The normal type has uniform discharge from each orifice without spreading.

Washer fluid

Washer fluid consists of anti-freeze (isopropyl alcohol, ethylene glycol or methanol) added to a detergent and an anticorrosive agent. The fluid used must not damage the rubber blade, weather stripping or body paint.

Wiper switch

The windshield wiper switch, located on the side of the steering column, is driver's input to activate windshield wipers and washer pump.

Today's windshield wipers can include an intermittent or delay function which causes the wiper to swipe the windshield periodically, rather than continuously. The driver can choose the length of time between swipes by adjusting a knob on the windshield wiper lever. Prior to the invention of intermittent wipers in the 1960's, cars usually had high and low speed continuous wipers (mist type), so the switch would allow the driver to vary the speed at which the wiper motor moves the windshield wipers only in this way. Intermittent wipers function by varying resistance in the wiper circuit. More resistance means a longer delay time.

DOOR LOCK MECHANISM

MECHANICAL LOCKING SYSTEM

In purely mechanical locking systems, each door or lid had an independent mechanism which could be operated from the outside with a key or from the inside with a knob.

Door assembly consists of catch, pawl and latch. The door lock striker is attached to the body pillar. Under closing operation the door lock striker gets caught by the latch and hold in the closed position and centres the door. The pawl positively locks the catch in position. To open the lock, the forces acting on inner or outer door handle are transferred to the pawl and cause the catch release to open the door. The door lock striker stays in the position while the catch swivels go into an open position.

POWER DOOR LOCKING

With power door locks, each door need not be locked manually. After all people board in to the car, if the driver pulls the locking lever of his door all the doors get locked and vice versa.

The power door lock actuator is positioned below the latch. A rod connects the actuator to the latch, and another rod connects the latch to the knob that sticks up out of the top of the door.

When the actuator moves the latch up, it connects the outside door handle to the opening mechanism. When the latch is down, the outside door handle is disconnected from the mechanism so that it cannot be opened.

CENTRAL LOCKING SYSTEM

The central locking system allows all doors, including the boot lid, to be locked simultaneously when the driver's door lock is activated. And inversely if the door of the driver side is open then all doors open. The locking system is operated with a key or remote control.

For convenience and safety reasons, mechanical latches allow each door to be unlocked manually from inside the car.

Central locking systems have electric locking systems in today's vehicles. Most of these combine a key with infrared or wireless remote control. This means that they can be triggered remotely, i.e. without contact between key and vehicle. Today, most vehicle manufacturers only fit a lock which can be operated with a key in one door, so the car can be unlocked in an emergency. The very latest systems enable entirely keyless vehicle access. Drivers only need to have the transmitter in their pockets, for example. The doors are then unlocked when the driver touches a door handle which has a built-in contact point.

The locking system comprises the following components:

Door handle/Handle strip

The door handle is the traditional means by which a vehicle is opened and closed from inside or outside. The external door strip usually houses the door lock. Door strips are increasingly used as design elements in modern cars. They can be chrome-plated or paint-finished in the same colour as the vehicle.

Door lock/Actuator

The latching mechanism in a vehicle is installed directly in its doors. It contains both a latch and an electric motor (actuator) which controls the central locking. The latch opens or closes the doors, whereas the door lock locks or unlocks the vehicle. Today, all door latches are powered by electric drives.

Fuel filler cap

The fuel filler cap must securely seal the fuel tank. Some fuel filler caps have locks, others do not. Fuel filler caps with locks are usually found on vehicles which have either a fuel filler flap which does not lock or no fuel filler flap at all. Fuel filler caps without locks are found on vehicles whose fuel filler flap is locked automatically via the central locking system.

Transponder

The transponder is usually integrated inside the key bow. It is the means by which the electronic immobiliser identifies that the correct key is being used. The transponder's code is read out as the key nears the ignition lock. If the code is correct, the electronic immobiliser sends the start enable to the engine.

Remote control

Remote controls are being used with increasing frequency in small cars, replacing the functions of a conventional key to all intents and purposes. A signal transmitter sends a signal or a coded order instruction to a receiver inside the vehicle, which usually controls a number of functions. Infrared remote controls have a range of up to 15 m. They rely on direct "visual" contact between transmitter and receiver. Today, infrared remote controls are only used rarely as they have been overtaken by other technologies. Wireless remote controls transmit on radio frequencies and have a range of up to approximately 100 m.

Keys

The basic function of keys and remote controls is the locking and unlocking of doors, luggage compartments, fuel filler caps, etc. they are also used to control the interior lighting and electronic immobiliser, the alarm system and the window lifters. The keys comprise two units: the milled, toothed key blade and the key bow. The latter is home to an increasing number of electronic functions such as the remote control for the central locking system or the boot lid.

Start/stop system

Traditionally, a vehicle key was needed to unlock the steering lock and to start the engine. Subsequently, the vehicle key was enhanced with the addition of a transponder based release mechanism for the electronic immobiliser. Today, keyless systems are increasingly being used to start engines. In a keyless system, a transmitter– which usually also houses the controller for the central locking – is inserted into a reader in the vehicle and the engine is then started by pressing a button. A more recent development has seen the use of systems that work without any contact at all. Here, it is sufficient to simply "take along" the transmitter (carrying it in a trouser pocket, for example) and press the pedals before starting the engine by pressing a button.

Steering lock

Steering locks have been a mandatory requirement set by insurance companies since 1969. They provide protection against theft. They are the means by which the steering column is unlocked and the engine is started – either electrically or in by conventional mechanical means.

Safety

Modern locking systems help to increase both security and safety in vehicles. Where security is concerned, they provide protection against theft and, in conjunction with an alarm system, act as a deterrent. In terms of safety, the integrated control of lighting elements when doors are unlocked, for example, contributes to safety on the road by improving the visibility of open doors.

Environmental protection

In the event of an accident, fuel filler caps with locks, which are also available for retrofitting, improve both safety and the protection of the environment by preventing fuel from escaping. Moreover, the valve systems installed in modern fuel filler caps reduce fuel evaporation. In the field of commercial vehicles too, locking systems make an active contribution to the protection of the environment, as they provide an assurance of safety for urea tanks. Urea is used to meet the strict environmental standards of Euro IV and V and to reduce the toxic emissions of diesel vehicles.

KEYLESS ENTRY

Most cars today come with the following keyless entry systems that can be used to turn on cars remotely.

Types of keyless entry	Features
Programmable keypad	Access car without by using a passcode.
Key fob	Unlock and lock doors; open trunk with touch of button, alarm activation, unique to each car.
Smart key	Unlock and lock doors; open trunk, and start car without a traditional key; unique to each car; each driver can have unique key with setting programmed.

BENEFITS

The Benefits of key fobs and remote entry systems in vehicles are:

1. Convenience
2. Safety
3. Customizable options

PROGRAMMABLE KEYPAD

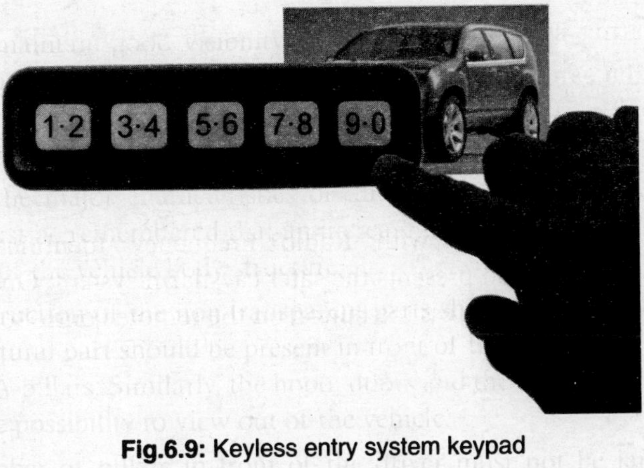

Fig.6.9: Keyless entry system keypad

Programmable keypad permits the driver to unlock the car door and/or release the trunk lid (luggage compartment) without a key. It consists of five touch buttons located on the driver's door belt molding.

Each button has two numbers, 1-2, 3-4, 5-6, 7-8, 9-10 and all are connected to a microcomputer for 'code' and 'sequence' identification.

Two five-digit codes are available, one code is programmed at the factory and cannot be changed, the other code is for owner programming and can be changed at any time. Entry into the car is gained by pressing the proper buttons in the proper sequence. For night time use, pushing any of the five buttons will illuminate all of the buttons, the interior car lighting system and the key lock light. The driver can then unlock the door by the use of a key, in the conventional manner, or by using either of the two codes-factory or owner programmed.

KEY FOB

Fig.6.10: Key fob

A key fob is a palm-sized portable device capable of controlling various parts of a car. Their primary function is to manage the remote-entry system installed in a car.

Aside from locking and unlocking car doors, some key fobs can:

- Pop the trunk latch
- Remotely start the vehicle ignition
- Arm/disarm a security system
- Activate the panic alarm
- Control automatic windows

SMART KEY

SmartCARD keyless entry with Radio Frequency Identification (RFID) technology and encryption presents the safer car alarm system. One can access a car without even a need to press the button on the remote control or take out any key from bag or pocket.

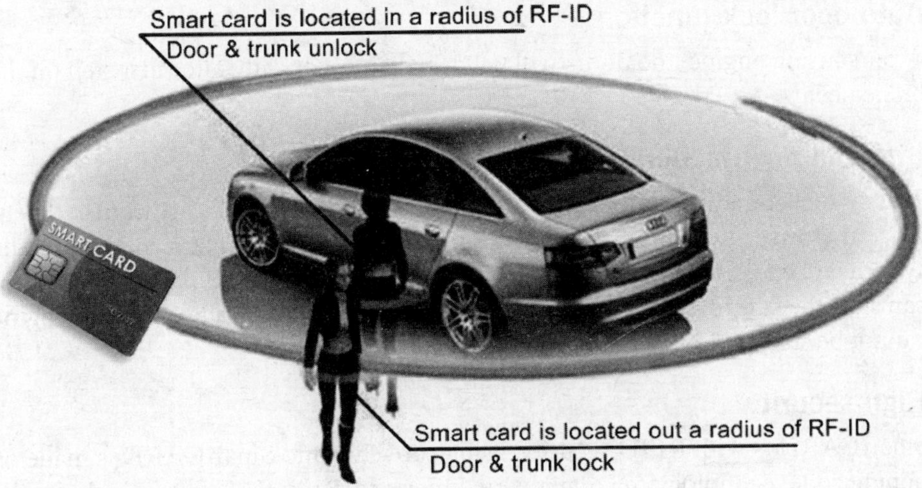

Fig.6.11: Smart key

MAIN FEATURES

The important features of this system are:

AUTO Door Close

If driver with SmartCARD is apart 1.5~2.0m from the car, the door will be closed automatically and it will enter into security mode. At this time, LED indicator will flicker in blue and red light in order.

AUTO Door Open

If driver with SmartCARD approaches to the car within 1.5~2.0m, the system recognises the validity of the card and door will be opened if its code matches. At this time, LED indicator will flicker in BLUE light.

Door open alarm

If the SmartCARD is apart and door is opened, the system will trigger the alarm sound and hazard light will flicker to notify that door is opened.

Slim smart key

SmartCARD is very thin and size is about two third of general credit card size. It is convenient to carry and keep. Therefore it is safe and convenient to no risk to lose.

Battery replacement time notification

If the battery of the SmartCARD is low, the system will notify the driver by alarm sound and flickering. At this time, battery should be replaced. (It can last for up to two more weeks after notification).

Auto door lock function

After starting engine, the doors will be locked automatically after first step on the brake pedal.

Immobilizer function

This system contains immobilizer function. It provides best security from car theft. Once the driver with SmartCARD approaches the car, the main module of the system will check the ID of the SmartCARD. In case of valid SmartCARD, driver can start the car. In case of invalid SmartCARD, the alarm will sound and engine cannot be started.

High security

SmartCARD is with RFID security, using core chip and SmartCARD is made of hoping code technology making it very difficult to copy.

BONNET RELEASE MECHANISM

With the vehicle parked, pull the release handle to unlock the bonnet. Insert your hand into the bonnet opening, slide the latch lever to the right, and lift up the bonnet.

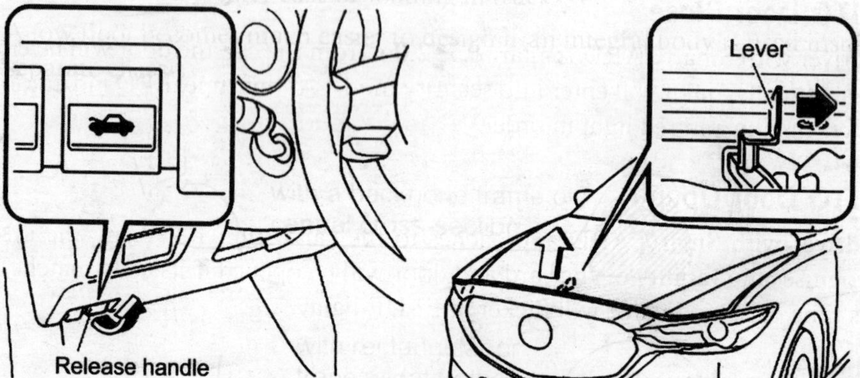

Fig.6.12: Bonnet release mechanism

BODY WORKING TOOLS

Body working tools include some very familiar general-purpose metal working tools as well as specialized tools only used in auto body repair. The following is a description of the most commonly used body working tools.

HAND TOOLS

HAMMERS

A number of different hammers are useful in the body shop. Many are specially shaped for a specific metal shaping operation.

BALL PEEN HAMMERS

The ball peen hammer is used for straightening bent underpinnings, smoothing heavy gauge parts, and roughly shaping body parts before work with a body hammer and dolly begins.

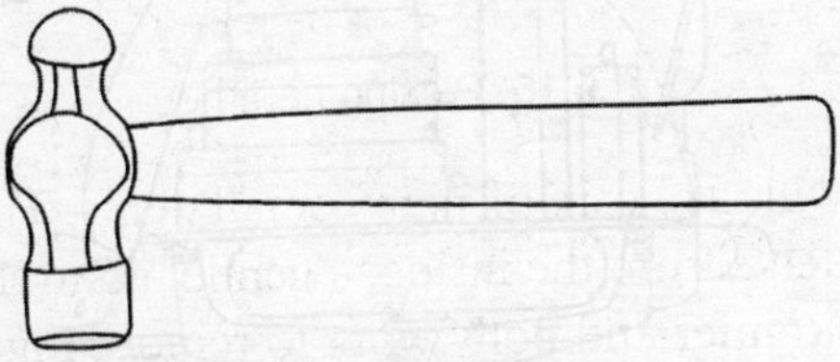

Fig.6.13: Ball peen hammer

Mallets

The rubber mallet gently bumps sheet metal without damaging the painted finish.

A steel hammer with rubber tips is another mallet useful in bodywork. The soft-faced hammer is used to work chrome trim and other delicate parts without marking the finish.

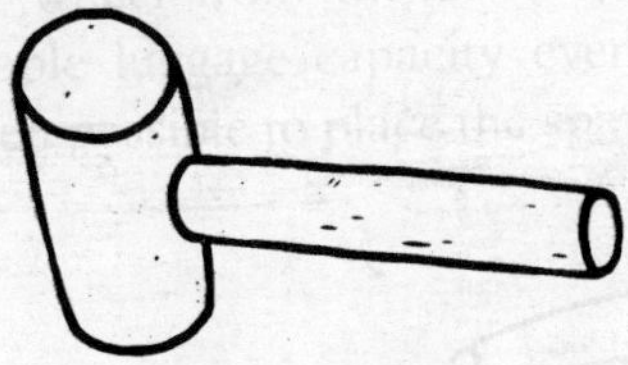

Fig.6.14: Mallet

Sledge hammer

A light sledgehammer is an essential tool for the first stages of re-forming damaged sheet metal. It should weight 3 to 5 pounds and have a short handle so that it can be used in tight places.

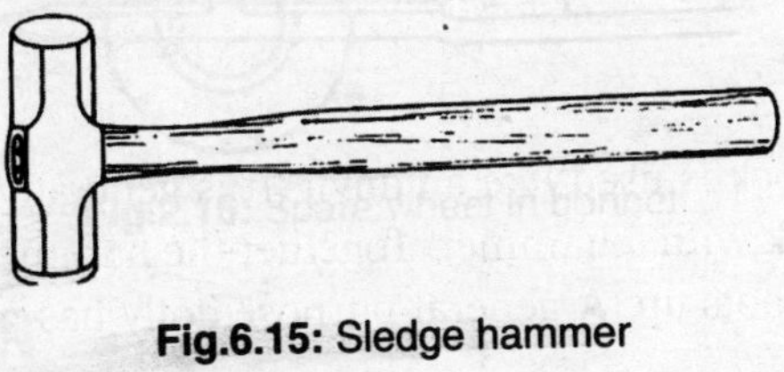

Fig.6.15: Sledge hammer

BODY HAMMERS

Body hammers are the basic tools for pounding sheet metal backs into shape. They come in many different designs such as flat, square heads and rounded heads.

Picking hammers

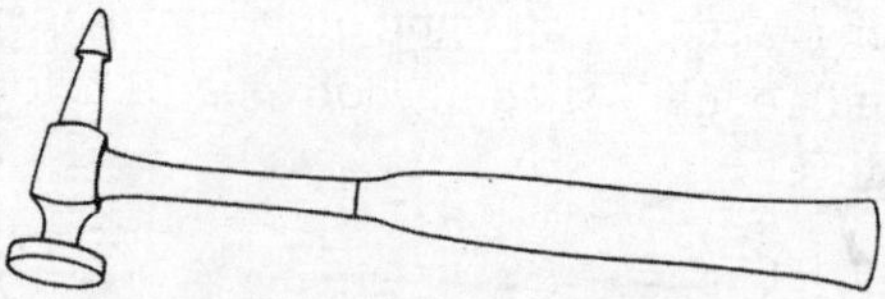

Fig.6.16: Picking hammer

The picking hammer will take care of many small dents. The pointed end is used to hammer out small dents from the inside; a gentle tap in the centre usually does it. The flat end is for hammer-and-dolly work to remove high spots and ripples.

Bumping hammers

Larger dents require the use of a bumping hammer bumping hammers can have round face or a square face. The surfaces of the faces are nearly flat. The faces are large area. These hammers are used for initial straightening on dented panels or for working inner panels that require more force but not a finish appearance.

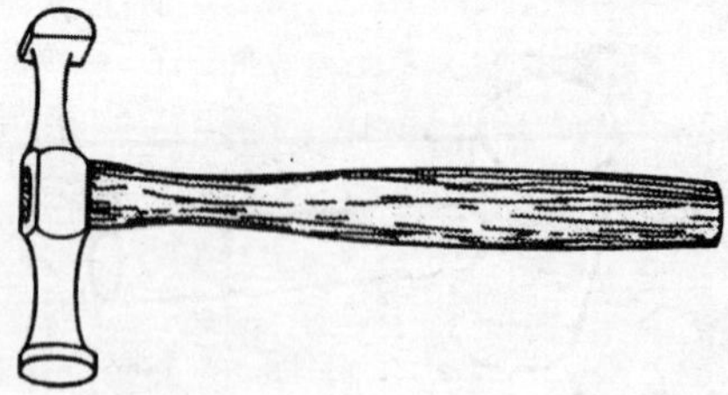

Fig.6.17: Bumping hammer

Finishing hammers

After the bumping hammer is used to remove the dent, final contour is achieved with the finishing hammer. The faces on a finishing hammer are smaller than those of the heavier bumping hammer. The surface of the face is crowned to concentrate the force on top of the ridge or high spot.

DOLLIES

The dolly or dolly block is used like an anvil. It is generally held on the backside of a panel being struck with a hammer. Together the hammer and dolly work high spots down and low spots up. A general-purpose dolly has many contours.

Fig.6.18: Low-crown dolly

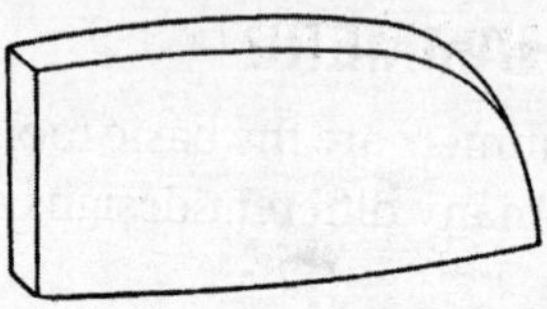

Fig.6.19: Toe dolly

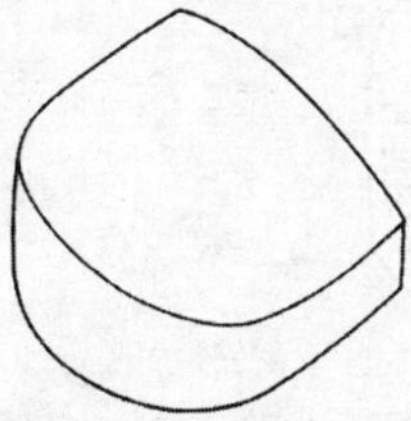

Fig.6.20: Heel dolly

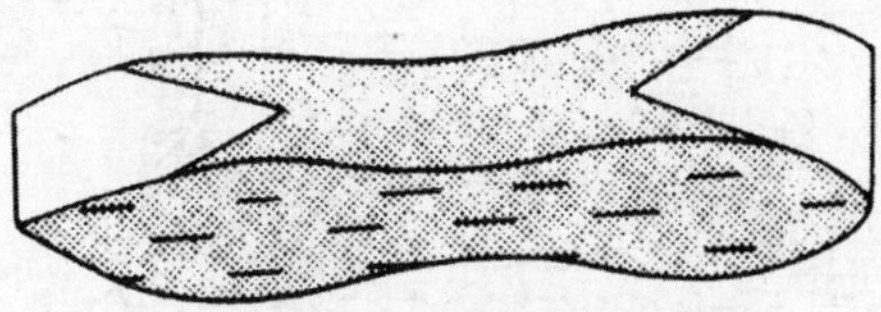

Fig.6.21: Beading dolly

SPOON

Body spoons are another class of body working tools that are used sometimes like a hammer and sometimes like a dolly. They are particularly useful on crease and ridges. A spoon dolly can be used as a dolly where the space behind a panel is limited. A dinging spoon is used with a hammer to work down ridges Inside spoons can used to pry up low places or can be struck with a hammer to drive up dents. Bumping files have serrated surfaces and are used to slap ridges or the underside of creases to bump the metal back to its original shape.

PICKS

Picks like spoons, are used to reach in to confined spaces. The pick is used only to pry up low spots. They vary in length and shape and most have a U- shaped end that serves as a handle picks are commonly used to rise low spots in door, quarter panels, and other sealed body sections Picks are often preferred to slide hammers and pull rods because they do not require drilling holes in the sheet metal.

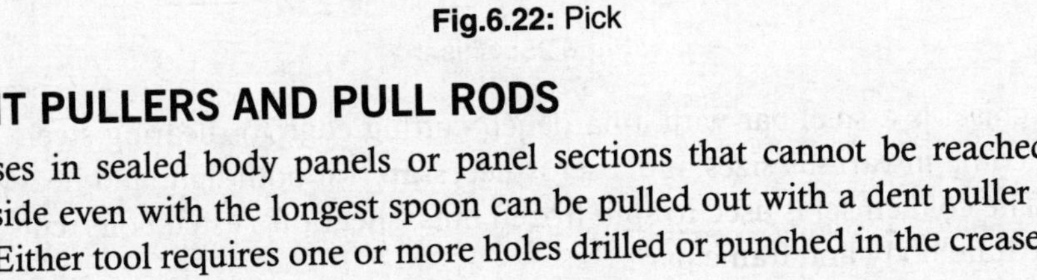

Fig.6.22: Pick

DENT PULLERS AND PULL RODS

Creases in sealed body panels or panel sections that cannot be reached from backside even with the longest spoon can be pulled out with a dent puller or pull rod. Either tool requires one or more holes drilled or punched in the crease.

SUCTION CUPS

The suction cup is a simple tool that recovers original body shape from shallow dents if they are not locked-in by a crease in the metal. Simply attach the suction cup to the centre of the dent and pull. The dent might come right out with no damage to the paint and no refinishing required.

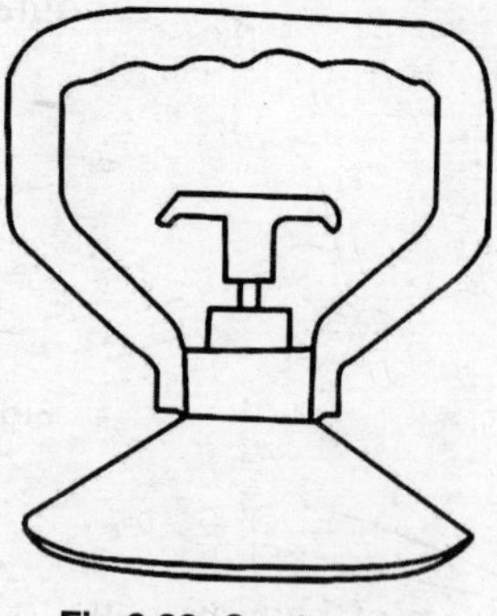

Fig.6.23: Suction cup

PUNCHES AND CHISELS

A good set punches and chisels are absolutely in every body working tool chest.

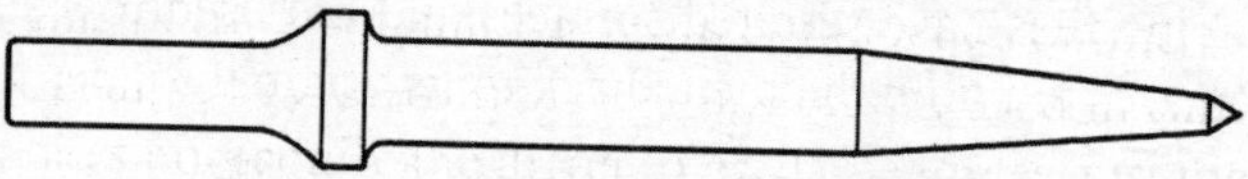

Fig.6.24: Punch

Centre punches are used to mark the location of parts before they are removed and for marking a spot drilling. A drifter or starter punch has a tapered point with a flat end that is used to drive out rivets, pins and bolts. A pin punch is similar to the drifter except its shaft is not tapered; thus it can be used to drive out smaller rivets or bolts. An aligning punch is a long tapered punch used to align body panels for welding or other body parts (such as fender bolt holes and a bumper).

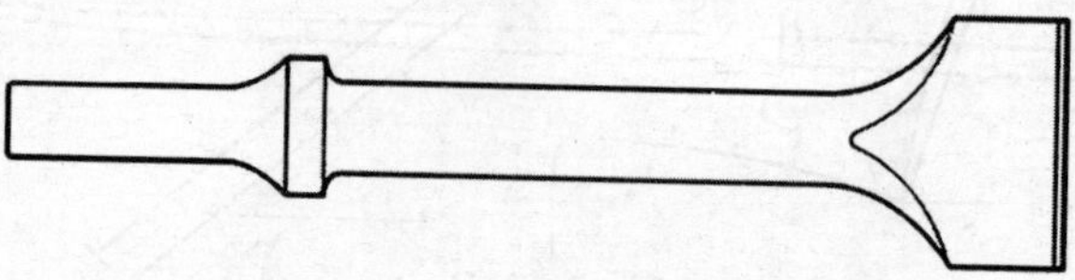

Fig.6.25: Chisel

A chisel is a steel bar with a hardened cutting edge for hearing steel. These chisels come in various sizes and a set is necessary for both light and heavy-duty work. The cold chisel is used to split frozen nuts, shear off rusted bolts, cut welds, and separate body and frame parts.

SCRATCH AWL

A scratch awl is used to pierce holes in their metal when a specific size hole is not required. It is also used to mark metal for cutting drilling or fastening. A hammer can be used to lightly drive the awl through heavier metal.

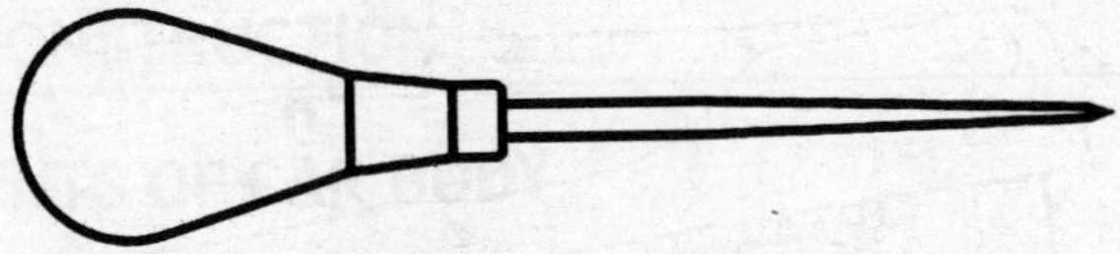

Fig.6.26: Scratch Awl

METAL CUTTTING SHEARS

Most body repair technicians have at least one pair of shears or tin snips. Snips are used to trim panels or metal pieces to size. Several types of metal cutters are useful.

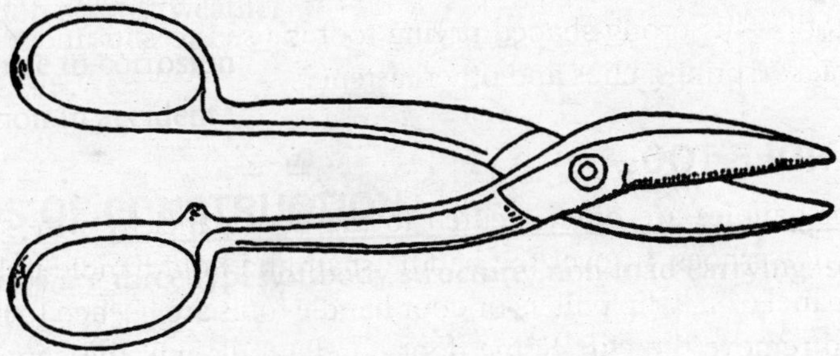

Fig.6.27: Metal cutting shear

Tin snips

Tin snips are perhaps on most common metal cutting tool. They can be used to cut straight or curved shapes in heavy steel.

Metal cutters

Metal cutters also called aviation snips, are used to cut through hard metals such as stainless steel. The narrow profile of jaws allows the snip to slip between the cut metal. The jaws are serrated to cut through the tough metal.

Panel cutters

Panel cutters are special snips used to cut through body sheet metal. These are used to make straight or curved cut outs in panels that require spot repair for rust or damage. They are designed to leave a clean, straight edge that can be easily welded.

RIVET GUN

Pop rivets are one of the handiest inventions for auto bodywork. They can be inserted into a blind hole through two pieces of metal and then drawn up with a riveting gun. The most commonly used rivets in bodywork are 1/8- and 3/16 inch.

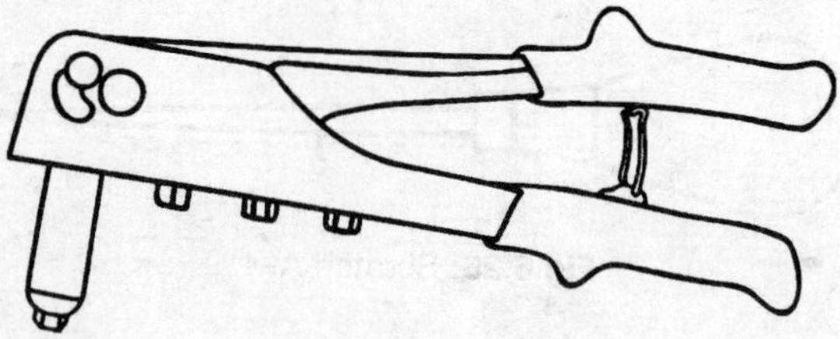

Fig.6.28: Rivet gun

TRIM AND UPHOLSTERY TOOLS

Any repair work that requires removing interior trim will be facilitated with an upholstery tool. This prong-shaped prying tool is used to slip under and pry up upholstery tacks, springs, clips and other fasteners.

DOOR HANDLE TOOL

Interior door handles are often secured to the door panel by wire spring clips. Shaped like horseshoes, fit over the handle shaft and hold handle tightly against the interior panel trim. Clip pullers or door handle tools are needed to reach inside the door and remove the clip. Some door handle tools pull the clip put: Others push the clip off the shaft.

BODY SURFACING TOOLS

A number of surfacing tools are used to give a repair its final and contour. Some are used to shape the repaired metal. Others are used to apply and shape plastic body filler and putty.

METAL FILES

After working a damaged panel back to its approximate original contour, a metal file is used to remove any remaining high spots. Two special files are necessary for most bodywork.

Reveal file

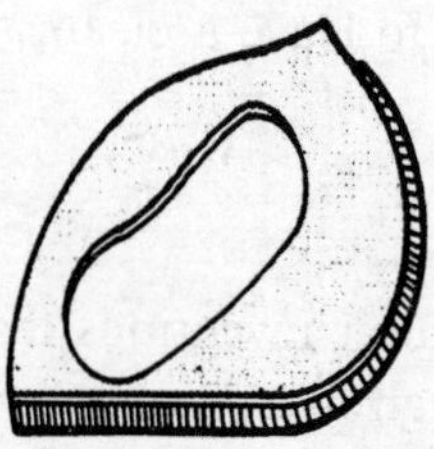

Fig.6.29: Reveal file

The reveal file is a small file that is available in numerous shapes. Generally it is curved to fit tightly crowned areas such as around windshields, wheel openings, and other panel edges. The reveal file is pulled, not pushed, when used. Pushing causes the file to chatter, resulting in nicks and an uneven surface.

Body files

Body files are used to level large surfaces. After a dent has been bumped or pulled back in to shape, the body file will hone down high spots and reveal any low spots that might require additional bumping. Keep in mind that it is possible to file through thin metal used in some vehicles.

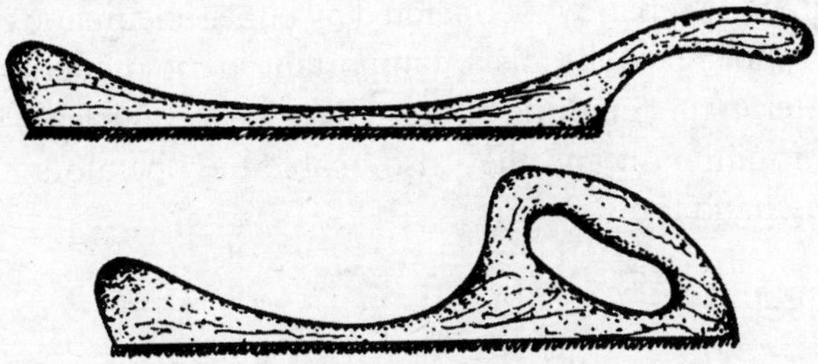

Fig.6.30: Body file

The blade of the body file is held in a flexible holder with a turnbuckle. The turnbuckle can be adjusted to flex the file. The flexible holder allows the shape of the file to fit the contour of the panel.

Fixed file holders are also available for filling flat or slightly convex shapes.

Surform file

Body filler can be made level to the adjacent panel with a surform file commonly referred to as a "cheese grater," the surform file is used to shape body filler while it is semi hard. Shaping the filler before it hardness shortens the waiting period while the filler cures and reduces the sanding effort later in the repair process.

Speed file

Once the body filler has hardened, the repair can be a shaped and levelled with a speed file is a rigid wooden holder about 17 inches long and 2-3/4 inches wide. Also called a flat boy, the speed file allows a repair area to be sanded quickly with long, level strokes. This eliminates waves and uneven areas.

The lightweight aluminium sander is designed to quickly level body filler. The extra long length helps avoid creating a waxy surface. The sander also flexes to match the panel contour. Adhesive backed sandpaper is applied from a roll. This particular sander can also be attached to a straight-line air sander.

Spreaders and squeegees

Spreaders and squeegees are two important tools used in auto body resurfacing. Spreaders are used to apply body filler. Spreaders are made of rigid plastic and are available in various sizes. Be sure to use one that is large enough to apply plastic filler over the repair area before the filler begins to set up.

A squeegee is a flexible rubber block approximately 2 inches by 3 inches and 3/16 inch thick. Squeegees are used to apply glazing putty and light coats of body filler. They are also used when wet sanding to skim water and sanding girt from the repair area.

POWER TOOLS

The tools used in body repair work operated by either pneumatic or electric power are called power tools. Power tools are important in the modern techniques used by the panel beater in the repairing of crash damage to vehicles. Their use reduces repair times to a minimum and they also enable the operators to achieve better results than using hand tools.

Air power chisel

The air power chisel is designed for the removal of damaged panels so that essential stripping can be carried out easily and quickly.

Metal shears

Metal shears are operated either electrically or by compressed air.

The machine is based on the principle of shearing metal, and this is done by a pair of very narrow blades, one of which is usually fixed while the other moves to and fro from the fixed blade at high speed. The blades have a very pronounced angle or set to permit the blade to pierce the sheet for internal cutting.

The shears are capable of cutting sheet metal up to a maximum of 2 mm (14 gauge) or 3 mm (10 gauge) aluminium, which more than covers the automobile requirements. The shear is used extensively in the cutting of light materials for the construction of new vehicles, but also plays an important role in the removal of damaged sections in crash repairs, as it leaves a nice neat cut and there is no risk of flame damage as with the more traditional methods of oxy-acetylene cutting.

Metal cutting nibbler

The metal cutting nibbler is a portable nibbler which uses a punch and die. The actual cutting is done by the edge of the punch which is reciprocated at high speed, leaving a slot or channel in the metal.

Power saw

The power saw is a high-speed pneumatic tool using interchangeable, reciprocating hacksaw blades. It is able to cut from straight lines to tight curves.

The tool can be used to cut a wide variety of materials including light-gauge steel, aluminium, reinforced glass fibre, wood and hardboard. Its fine cut is ideally suited for panel replacement where joints have to be cut and welded. Another power saw is the rotary or circular saw.

POWER DRILL

There are two types of power drill used in the body shop. The majority are usually electrically driven and require a 13 A electrical power point, while the others are air powered and require a compressor and air points. The most popular sizes in common use are the 10 mm pistol drill and 19 mm heavy-duty machines. Drills are used mostly for drilling out spot welds along damaged panels which need removing, and also for drilling out broken rivets and bolts.

SANDING MACHINE

Sanders are the most frequently used power tools in the body repair shop.

Disc sander

The disc sander is the most popular sander. It is a powerful machine with a hard rubber flexible pad on to which the actual sanding disc is fastened by means of a centre nut. Disc sanders are driven either electrically or by compressed air.

The main uses of the disc sander in the repair shop are sanding sections on panels which are either rusted or have been repaired by planishing and require sanding to a smooth finish in readiness for painting; cleaning sections that need to be filled with solder prior to tinning; stripping paint prior to planishing or dressing out; dressing off surplus weld metal after welding new sections; feather edging minor paint blemishes; and blending in body solder or plastic filler in sections that have been filled.

Belt sander

The belt sander can be used for repair to bodywork, and is extremely good on convex or concave surfaces where access with a disc sander would be difficult.

Pneumatic sander/filer

The pneumatic sander/filer is a dual-purpose tool for either sanding or filing.

Geared orbital sander/polisher

The geared orbital sander/polisher is a multi-orbital action machine which eliminates swirl marks and allows coarse grit paper to be used for high stock removal rates. On paint and fibreglass it leaves a perfect key for primers. The multi-orbital action reduces work surface heat generation, which is particularly important when sanding fillers and paint. The tool can also be used for polishing because of its rotary gearing.

Angle grinder

The small angle grinder is sometimes known as a mini-grinder or a grinderette. It is a versatile one-handed machine, and will cut away damaged metal, remove rust, grind down spot, MIG and gas welds, smooth in-fills and generally grind down prepared surfaces.

POLISHER/BUFFERS

An air polisher is used to smooth and shine painted surfaces by spinning a soft buffing pad. Polishing or buffing compound is rubbed over the paint with the polisher pad. This removes minor paint imperfections to increase paint gloss (shine).

PANEL REPAIR

Two repair methods can be followed in repairing any damaged panel: One procedure is to straighten only those portions of the permanent damage. The relatively undamaged areas will then recover to original shape. This is the Fairmount method. The other method is to get inside the damaged area with a heavy hammer, or other tool, and beat or push the whole area out roughly to shape. This is the "rough-'em-out smooth-' em-up" method.

The drawback of Rough-'em-out-smooth-'em-up" method are as follows.

- always causes additional damage to the panel
- excessive amount of additional and unnecessary repair work
- consumes more time
- not easier to perform.

FAIRMOUNT METHOD

The Fairmount method has three phases: analysis, metal bumping, and metal finishing.

Analysis

From analysis, the mechanical operations of bumping and finishing are planned so that they are simplified and shortened. Analysis is a simple operation for an experienced technician. He notes the location of direct damage, the direction from which the damaging force came and the extent of the indirect damage.

He also determines whether and how much the reinforcing members of the body or fender are bent, and most important, the probable sequence in which the ridges and V-channels were formed as the damage occurred.

Metal bumping

Metal bumping is the mechanical phase in which the repairman restores the damaged panel, or panels, approximately to their original shape. Welding, shrinking, and torch soldering are a part of this phase of body and fender repair.

Metal finishing

The third phase, metal finishing, is the process of preparing the metal-bumped surface for fine, smooth appearance, ready for repainting. The metal-bumped areas are filed, disc ground, and sanded smooth. Minor imperfections are smoothed by raising or lowering to exact level. Minute imperfections are filed or sanded to a precision job. When this phase is complete, the outside surface of the panel is as smooth as when new and is ready to be repainted.

MINOR BODY REPAIRS

Repairing scratches

Most vehicles brought in to the auto body shop for damage repair and or refinishing have a variety of minor imperfections in the paint. Some defects such as chalking or scuffmarks can be removed with rubbing compound. The abrasive compound removes the damaged surface paint and brings out the luster in the paint beneath. Other defects, such as scratches are too deep to buff out with rubbing compound. If the scratch penetrates through the primer and exposes the metal underneath, the technique for repairing nicks and chips is used. But shallow scratches that are too deep to be buffed out, but do not reach the metal underneath the paint, can be filled with putty or a polyester primer-surfacer before painting.

Repairing nicks

Minor bumps and scrapes often leave nicks and scratches in car's finish. A stone thrown up by a passing vehicle can chip the paint. Exposing the sheet metal beneath. Sideswipe collisions result in scrapes and gouges. Any time bare metal is exposed to the air, rust formation must be inhibited with primer before new finish is applied.

After the repair area is cleaned and dewaxing the first step in repairing nick or deep scratch is sanding the ragged edges of the chipped point to a smooth surface. This is commonly referred to as feather edging. Featheredging tapers the edges of the paint so that is gradually blends in with the metal surface. After the nicked paint edges are sanded to a smooth surface, clean the metal with metal conditioner. Finally sanding and priming are necessary to achieve a super smooth surface.

Repairing dings

One kind of surface imperfection that sometimes requires minor metal work in addition to filling is a ding. Dings are small dents often caused by carelessly opened doors, when a panel is struck by the edge of another car, door, the impact creates a shallow depression in the metal. This small tension area is also usually accompanied by a pressure ridge surrounding the ding.

To repair ding:

- Wash and dewax the surface
- Grind the finish from the repair area with light weight air grinder
- After removing the paint from the repair area, file down the ridge around the ding.
- Apply a skim coat of body filler
- The surrounding paint edges must be feather edged.

Repairing rust damage

Corrosion damage on vehicle panels takes two forms: surface rust and rust outs. Surface rust in its early stage can simply leave a reddish coating on the metal surface. Given time, the rust will cut pits into the surface. Eventually the pitting will develop in to holes, or rust outs. Both types of damage require different repair procedures. These are outlined in the block diagram below.

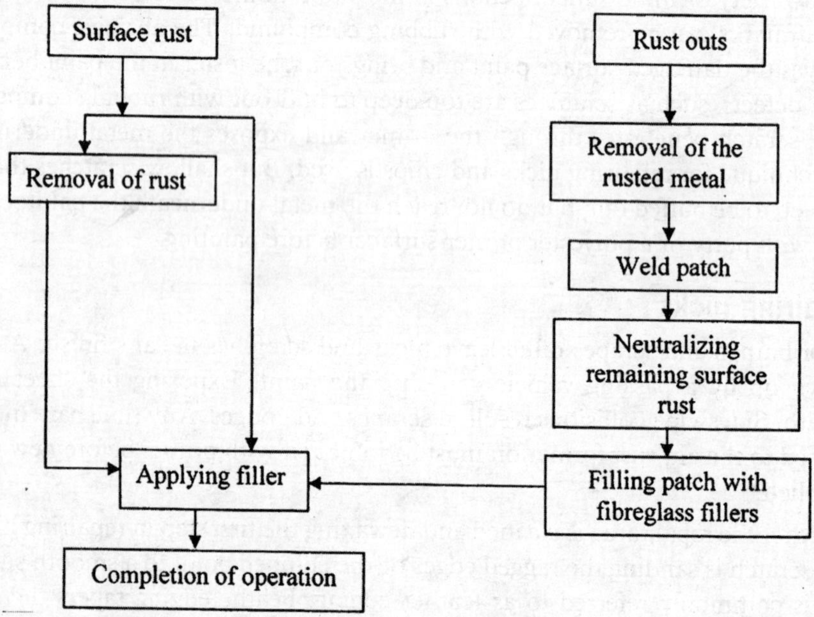

Fig.6.31: Rust repair procedure

REPAIRING PLASTICS

A car is made up of about 15% plastics material, by weight. Plastics materials are very light, so in terms of bulk the percentage is much larger. The plastics parts are often damaged in even a minor accident.

There are two methods of repairing plastics.

1. Bonding
2. Plastic welding

The two main classifications of plastics used in vehicles are: thermoplastics and thermosetting plastics. As a general rule thermoplastics can be welded and thermosets bonded.

BONDING

Adhesive repair systems are of two types: cyanoacrylate (CA) and two-part. Two-part is the most commonly used.

Cyanoacrylates

Cyanoacrylates (CAs), are one-part, fast-curing adhesives used to help repair rigid and flexible plastics. They are often used as a filler or to tack parts together before applying the final repair material. CAs are sometimes referred to as "super glues." CAs set up very quickly.

Two-part adhesive

Two-part adhesive systems consist of a base resin and a hardener (catalyst). The resin comes in one container and the hardener in another. When mixed, the adhesive cures into a plastic material similar to the base material in the part. Two-part adhesive systems are an acceptable alternative to welding for many plastic repairs. They are also stronger than CAs.

Repairs of minor cuts and cracks

Adhesives are usually used for repairing minor cuts and cracks in plastic parts. First, wash and clean the area to be bonded. The surfaces must be free of wax, dust, and grease. Allow the part(s) to warm to 70°F (21°C) before applying adhesives. The adhesive kit should have two elements: an accelerator and an adhesive. Spray one side of the crack with the accelerator. Then apply the adhesive to the same side of the crack. Carefully position the two sides of the cut or crack in their original position, and quickly press them together with firm pressure. Hold for a full minute to achieve good bond strength. Then allow the repair to cure for 3 to 12 hours for maximum strength.

Repairs of gouges, tears and punctures

The repair area must be absolutely clean for proper bond strength.

Prepare the repair adhesive material on a clean, flat, nonporous surface, such as metal or glass. Most adhesive compounds come in two tubes. Squeeze out equal amounts of the repair mix. Then, completely mix the two components until a uniform colour and consistency is achieved. Apply the adhesive into the hole, using a squeegee or plastic spreader. The adhesive material will begin to set in about 2 to 3 minutes. Two applications of the adhesive are usually required. When the adhesive repair material has dried, establish a contour to the surrounding area with a disc sander and a grit abrasive on a sanding block. When the final sanding is completed, the area is cleaned to remove all dust and loose material. The plastic surface is then ready to be painted.

PLASTIC WELDING

Plastic welding uses heat and sometimes a plastic filler rod to join or repair plastic parts. When welding plastics, the materials are fused together by the proper combination of heat and pressure.

Dashboards and some flexible bumper assemblies which are made from thermoplastics can be welded. There are two ways of welding thermoplastics. One is to use a hot air welding gun and the other is to use a soldering iron. The hot air welding gun blows out a stream of air (the temperature is over 100°C) which will melt the plastic. The paint should be cleaned off about 20 mm on both sides of the joints. The welded joint is made using the blow gun and a plastics filler rod.

Thin thermoplastic items which will melt with less heat can be welded using a soldering iron (without the solder).

If the component, say a bumper, has been holed, it is possible to weld in a piece from a scrap bumper of the same shape. Cut the damaged section out of the bumper, a round or oval shape will prevent further cracking. Then cut a piece out of the scrap bumper which will just fit into the hole. Remove the paint from all the edges and weld in using blow gun or soldering iron.

PLASTIC BODY FILLERS

Epoxy fillers (body fillers) are simple to use in that the body portions do not have to be straightened as closely as when making repairs without it. The advantage of using body filler lies in the fact that a badly damaged vehicle can be returned to a like-new appearance quickly and with a limited amount of metal straightening. Additional, the use of thinner metals in the bodies of modern vehicles makes it difficult to reform panels into their original shape.

Most auto body repairs require some application of plastic body filler. Plastic body filler is fast and inexpensive way to restore the final counter of a damaged panel. According to the manufacturer's instructions, body filler can be applied over rough places and form it with a body file or sanding until it conforms to the desired contour.

Before any filler is applied, the damaged panel should be returned to its correct shape and dimensions by bumping, stretching and pulling more over all holes, cracks and joint gaps must be welded and brazed. Some body fillers are hygroscopic which means they absorb moisture when exposed to humid conditions.

Body fillers and putties can also be used to repair minor defects such as dings, stone chips, surface rust and rust outs.

CHEMICALLY HARDENING FILLERS (PLASTIC FILLERS)

- These fillers are used in the body repair trade as an alternative method to body soldering.
- They are based on the polyester group of thermosetting resins, and require a catalyst or activator to cure them.
- When they are mixed together a catalytic action takes place, resulting in the filler hardening very quickly.
- As this plastic filler does not require heat during its application it has certain clear advantage.
  - Its use eliminates fire risk, especially filling next to petrol tanks or any inflammable materials.
  - It also eliminated the problem of heat distortion which occurs when solder filling
  - It is cheaper than body solder and much easier to apply

Composition

Plastic body filler is very similar to paint in composition. Both are made of resins, pigments, and solvents. Most plastic body fillers have a polyester resin that acts as a binder. When the filler is applied and the solvent evaporates, the binders hold the pigments together in a tough, durable film. The basic pigment or filler in conventional fillers is talc.

Plastic fillers harden by chemical action. The chemical rxn is set off by oxygen. To speed up the process, the manufacturer provides a chemical catalyst. The catalyst, in liquid or cream form, is called hardener. Hardener is basically a chemical compound called peroxide.

As table 6.2 shows, the filler will soon become too stiff to work in just a few minutes after adding hardener, depending on the ambient air temper.

Table 6.2: Effect of temperature on working time

Temperature	Working times
100°F	3 to 4 minutes
85°F	4 to 5 minutes
77°F	6 to 7 minutes
70°F	8 to 9 minutes

Applying plastic body filler

1. Preparing the surface for filling
   - Wash the repair area to remove dirt.
   - Then clean the area with wax and grease remover.
   - Use # 24 or # 36 girt grinding disc to remove the paint and rust

2. Mixing the filler
   - Mix the can of filler to a uniform and smooth consistency before use, the filler in the upper portion of the can will be too him. This results in runs and sags in application, slow and poor curing, a summery condition when sanded
3. Kneading the hardener
   - Loosen the cap of the cream hardener tube to prevent the hardener from being or bound.
   - Knead the tube thoroughly to assure a smooth paste like consistency. Like tooth paste when squeezed out.
   - If the cream hardener is not kneaded thoroughly to produce a smooth, paste like consistency or ribbon-effect when squeezed out.
   - The hardener can cause slow and in effective curing
   - Poor adhesion
   - Blistering and peeling after recoating
   - Poor feather edge
4. Mixing filler and hardener
   - Using a clean putty or squeeze, place the filler on a smooth clean, nonporous surface such as sheet metal or glass
   - Add the hardener in the proportion indicated on the can instructions
   - With a clean putty knife or squeeze and using a scraping motion (back and forth). Mix the filler and the hardener together the thoroughly to achieve a uniform color
5. Applying Filler
   - Apply the mixed filler promptly a thoroughly clean and well- sanded surface. A first tight, thin application is recommended. Press firmly to force filler into sand scratches to minimize the bond. When cured, apply additional thicker application as needed to build up the repaired area to proper contour.
6. Shaping the filler
   - Allow the filler to cure to a semi hard consistency
   - This usually takes 15 to 20 minutes

PASSENGER COMPARTMENT SERVICE

During a major auto accident, the interior or passenger compartment of the vehicle is often damaged and must be repaired.

Interior trim service

When servicing trim pieces, remember these basic rules:

- Make sure all metal screws are removed from hidden areas before popping out plastic clips.
- Be careful not to break brittle plastic trim pieces. Do not use excessive force, which could bend or even break the panel. Use a forked trim tool to reach behind trim pieces to pry out all plastic clips. Pulling force should be applied to or near the head of the clip. This will avoid trim panel breakage.
- Disconnect the battery before disconnecting any wires in the passenger compartment. This will prevent a possible short circuit that could quickly burn up wiring.
- Keep all fasteners organized in plastic bags or cans.
- This will help you keep track of their locations and speed reassembly.
- Use a logical sequence of trim panel removal. Usually one trim piece overlaps and helps hold an adjacent panel. Remove the top trim piece first.

CORROSION

Corrosion is the deterioration of a metal as a result of chemical reactions between it and the surrounding environment.

There are three basic types of vehicle body corrosion: chemical, electrochemical and fretting.

Chemical corrosion

In chemical corrosion the metal is oxidized or attacked by other chemical substances. Chemical corrosion requires three elements

- Exposed metal
- Oxygen
- Moisture (electrolyte)

Electrochemical corrosion

In electrochemical corrosion a current is setup due to the presence of an electrolyte (which may be water, moisture or steam) which destroys the sheet surface.

Fretting corrosion

In fretting corrosion, metal surface rub against each other during vibration, and small particles are produced which harden and damage the two surfaces by indentation.

ANTICORROSION METHODS

A vehicle body is exposed to corrosion throughout its life and because the load-carrying structure determines the service life of the vehicle, it is essential that it be properly protected against such effects.

Corrosion can be prevented by three basic methods used on today's automobile.

- Improved materials
- Protective coating
- Correct design

Improved materials

Sheet metal material may have its corrosive properties improved by the addition of copper (0.2-0.5 percent). This addition increases the resistance to corrosion by 1.5-3.0 times. A small addition of chrome or molybdenum is even more advantageous. The cost of these additions compensates in the form of increased service life.

Protective coating

The most popular protective coating is phosphate, which is usually applied by dipping the body in a bath before painting. Internal parts are coated by bituminous sprays. Paraffin additives in the treatment of the sheets especially lower contact corrosion.

Galvanizing is the process of coating steel with zinc. It is one of the principal methods of corrosion protection applied during the manufacturing process. On galvanized steel, the zinc forms a natural barrier between the steel and the atmosphere.

Paint provides a barrier between the atmosphere and the steel surface. When this barrier is in place, the moisture and impurities in the air cannot interact with the steel surface and the steel is protected from corrosion.

Anticorrosion materials or agents can be divided in to three broad categories.

- Anticorrosion compounds: Either wax or petroleum based compounds are resistant to chipping and abrasion; they can undercoat, sound leaden and completely seal the surface of a car from the destructive causes of rust and corrosion. They should be applied to the under carriage and inside body panels so that they can penetrate in to joints and body crevices to form a pliable, protective film.
- Body sealer or sealant: This prevents the penetration of water or mud into panel joints and serves the important role of preventing rust from forming between adjoining surfaces.
- Antirust agents: They are used where it is difficult get unit corrosion material coverage. This includes such areas as the backsides of welded parts with boxed cross sectional structures such as side members and body pillars that cannot be painted.

Correct design

Correct design means the avoidance of joints which prove inaccessible for the protective coating as well as the avoidance of pockets which collect water. Joints between two metals are especially prone to corrosion. Thus plastics should be used as spacers between chromes surfaces and non-chromed steel sheets.

PAINING PROCESS

Auto refinishing or painting is a very important part of the auto repair business.

TOPCOAT or COLOUR COAT
SEALER COAT (OPTIONAL)
UNDERCOAT or PRIMER
METAL SURFACE OF AUTO BODY

Above shows the coatings of paint that are applied to a typical automobile. The undercoat, often called the prime coat, provides a bond between the base metal and the colour coats. When refinishing, a sealer coat might be used to prevent minor sand scratches from showing up and to provide a smoother finish. The topcoat is the actual colour coat that is applied to the body.

The topcoat is generally made up of three basic elements. First there is pigment, which gives the paint colour. The next element is the binder, which holds the pigment in liquid form and gives it strength and gloss. The binder allows the pigment to adhere to the surface being refinished. It is a clear finish. The third basic ingredient is the solvent, which is most often added by the painter just before the topcoat is used. Its main purpose is to make the pigment and binder less viscous and allow the paint to be sprayed. After spraying, the solvent evaporates, leaving the pigment and binder to make up the paint film on the auto body.

Clear coats are transparent and come in acrylic lacquer, acrylic enamel, enamel, and urethane. The clear coat is sprayed over the new finish and adds lustre to the finished product.

Polishing

Glazing or polishing involves using very fine grit compound to bring the paint surface up to full gloss. It is usually done after compounding. You can hand-polish small or hard-to-reach areas. Machines polish larger areas to save time.

Slight defects in the topcoat can be repaired by polishing. The choice of compounds depends on the extent of the damage. Final polishing should always be done with an ultrafine polishing compound.

When using rubbing compounds and machine glazes be sure to follow these procedures:

1. Use a single manufacturer's product line.
2. Follow the manufacturer's recommendations for use.
3. Use the materials sparingly.

4. Use the buffing wheel to evenly distribute the material over the area that is being repaired.
5. Keep the pad flat and directly over the surface being repaired.
6. Use a slow, methodical motion so you can keep track of how much area has been buffed.
7. Use the finest grit product possible last. Using a finer grit product may take a little longer initially but will generally require less time to complete the repair.
8. Reduce swirl marks by avoiding coarse products and worn buffing pads.

Instead of a circular action buffer, one should use an orbital action machine for final polishing. An orbital action polisher will move the polishing compound in a random manner to remove swirl marks from buffing.

PAINT PROBLEMS

Chalking

It is the progressive powdering of paint film on the painted surface. This occurs because of improper dispersion of pigment and vehicle.

Flaking

Peeling out of paint film from the painted surface is known as flaking. This is due to the presence of dust or greasy matter in the paint. Improper surface preparation may also cause this.

Cracking

Cracking of paint occurs because of (i) Unequal expansion and contraction of coats (ii) Variation of temperature of exposed film. This can be prevented by applying a primary hard coat.

Colour change

This happens because of chemical effects of atmospheric gases in the environment.

Review Questions

Short Questions

1. What is FRP? Indicate its merits and demerits as body material.
2. What are the salient features of FRP?
3. List out the body trim items.
4. What is meant by body trim and body upholstery?
5. Indicate the properties and uses of GRP as vehicle body material.

6. State the advantages of GRP.
7. What is meant by timber?
8. List at least four hand tools used in body panel repair.
9. What are the criteria for the selection of paint?
10. With a sketch illustrate a typical window winding mechanism.
11. How vehicle body gets corroded?

Long Questions

1. Explain the properties and uses of various materials that are being commonly used in the construction of vehicle bodies.
2. List out the different types of vehicle body corrosion and explain the step by step procedure of vehicle body painting process.
3. With a neat sketch explain the construction and working of door lock and window winding mechanism.
4. Explain the anti-corrosion methods with its applications.
5. Explain the painting process procedures for a modern car body.
6. Discuss the body repair filler material and their types.
7. Briefly explain various trim items used in a car.

Bibliography

1. J.Powleski, Vehicle Body Engineering, Century, 1970.
2. G.Devaradjane, Classic Support Material, IRTT.
3. Ronald W. Maze, Automotive Body Refinishing, MaGraw-Hill Book Company.
4. William C. Mann, Smart Tèchnology for Aging, Disability, and Independence: The State of the Science, John Wiley & Sons, 2005.
5. Joseph Katz, Automotive Aerodynamics, John Wiley & Sons, Ltd, 2016.
6. Rami Hughes, Automobile Safety Improvements: An Analysis, Xlibris Corporation, 2010.
7. Principles of Automotive Vehicles, United States. Dept. of the Army United States. Dept. of the Air Force, January 1956.
8. Code of Practice for Bus Body Design and Approval, ARAI Pune, 2008.

Index